Content Chemistry

An Illustrated Handbook for Content Marketing

BY ANDY CRESTODINA

ISBN: 978-0-9883364-3-8 (paperback)
ISBN: 978-0-9883364-4-5 (ebook)
ISBN 978-0-9883364-5-2 (mobibook)

Contents

INTRODUCTION

Welcome to Content Chemistry

This book is the result of thousands of conversations with hundreds of companies over the last 15 years. On January 1, 2000, I started the new century with a new career on the web. Since that day, I've immersed myself in nearly every aspect of digital marketing. In April 2001, I co-founded a web design company called Orbit Media Studios with my great friend Barrett Lombardo. Today, Orbit is an award-winning team of 40 specialists with hundreds of happy clients and over 1,000 successful projects.

Through all of that experience, I've learned many things about digital marketing. The book you're reading now is a compilation of the most important and effective lessons I've learned.

The simplest way to summarize all of it goes something like this...

To be successful, websites must do two things: 1) attract visitors, and 2) convert those visitors into leads and customers. In order to do this, web marketers must do two things: 1) create content, and 2) promote it. I've learned that content makes the difference between success and failure on the web.

By the time you finish reading this book, you should have a solid foundation of all the main topics as well as a good understanding of the specific actions you'll need to take to succeed on your own.

You'll know which actions lead to which outcomes. You'll know where you're going and how to get there.

Beyond this, my hope is that your new insights into web marketing will motivate you to get started and stay active. I hope you realize that web marketing is enjoyable because it's creative, something both social and analytical. There's nothing intimidating about it. You may discover that, yes, web marketing is critical to modern business, but it's also a lot of fun.

Andy Crestodina
Strategic Director, Orbit Media Studios
@crestodina | Google+ | LinkedIn

Who This Book is For

This book is for people who are interested in improving their marketing, increasing sales and growing their business. You don't need to be a social media celebrity or a best-selling author. You do need to be yourself. And regardless of who you are, it's almost certain that you're well suited for content marketing.

If you're a thoughtful, detail-oriented person who enjoys researching and writing well-considered articles, content marketing is for you. If you're a fast, informal writer who can produce quick posts based on today's news, content marketing is for you.

If you're analytical and prefer digging through data over chatting with people, content marketing is for you. If you're a social person who would rather connect with people than analyze numbers, content marketing is for you.

Introverts and extroverts, number-crunching researchers and big-picture thinkers—content marketing has something for everyone. However, you must write. All content marketers have this in common.

How to Use This Book: Experiment and Measure

This book is called "Content Chemistry" for a reason. As in chemistry, content marketing is about experimentation and measurement. Like a chemist, we'll mix chemicals (content), add energy (promotional activity) and observe and measure the reactions (analytics). Then we'll repeat or try something new.

- **Experimentation**: These practices will continue to evolve. Techniques should be adapted to suit your business. It's an ongoing process of trial and error and gradual improvement.

- **Measurement**: Virtually every aspect of web marketing is measurable, much more so than with traditional advertising. This is part of the fun, but also a necessary part of the work. *If you're not measuring results, you're not doing content marketing.*

Results will often be unexpected, but the purpose remains constant: we seek awareness, relevance and trust.

How This Book is Structured

This book is broken into two sections: Lecture and Lab. The Lecture section includes the theory of web marketing, which consists of attracting visitors (traffic) and getting them to take action (conversions). The Lab section covers web marketing in practice, which means creating content and promoting it.

There is no need to read this book cover to cover, so feel free to jump around. Each page has insights and ideas for you to try. Depending on your skill level, you may skim the Lecture section (Chapters 2 and 3) and go straight to the Lab section (Chapters 4 and 5).

The techniques in this book are intended to demonstrate the concepts. I have tried them all and found each to be successful. Once you understand both the theory and practice, I invite you to try a little chemistry of your own!

What is Content Marketing?

Content marketing is the art and science of pulling your audience toward your business. It is based on the concept that there are relevant prospects looking for your product or service right now. If you can connect with them, help them, and teach them, some of them will become loyal customers.

Content Marketers create and promote useful, relevant information with the goal of attracting and engaging website visitors, and then converting those visitors into leads and customers

We do this by creating, publishing and promoting content that is relevant to our clients and prospects. We use blogs, search engine optimization (SEO), social media and email marketing.

Content marketing is sensitive to the behaviors and psychology of potential buyers. Whether we're looking for jet engines or consulting services, a wedding DJ or a local florist, we are more likely than ever to look to the Internet before making a decision to act. Every day we search, research, read recommendations, and seek advice from experts.

Where traditional marketing aims to interrupt and distract, content marketing aims to attract and assist.

⚠ **CAUTION!** Content marketing is a slow process. Although the techniques in this book are things you can (and should) start doing today, the impact on sales and revenue may be months or years away. Many of the tactics are cumulative, such as increasing email subscribers, growing social followings and building links. Building up your content and audience takes time. Don't expect to get rich (or be relevant) overnight.

The Evolution of Marketing

To understand the future of marketing, we must first understand the past. Let's take a brief look at the history of marketing.

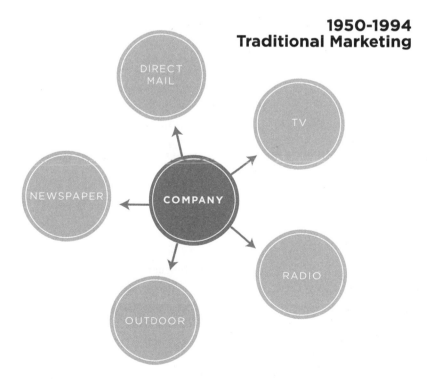

1950-1994 Traditional Marketing

DIRECT MAIL · TV · RADIO · OUTDOOR · NEWSPAPER · COMPANY

1950-2004
Traditional Marketing + Web

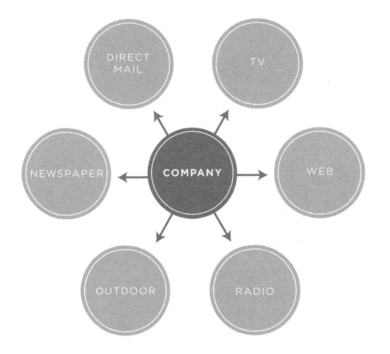

In the beginning...

Marketing was dominated by advertising and that meant buying media. It meant buying space in newspapers and hoping consumers would notice before they turned the page. It meant *buying time* on TV and hoping consumers would keep watching when the show cut to a commercial break.

Businesses sent postcards and letters to our homes and called us during dinner, pushing out their messages with whatever budget they could muster. They hoped that consistent, repeated distractions and interruptions would convince us to buy. Some businesses still do.

But that magazine ad had limited space and the TV commercial had precious little time. If the ad budget was cut, the message disappeared completely.

And it was always so hard to tell what was actually bringing in sales. There was an old saying among marketing executives: "I know I'm wasting half of my advertising budget, I just don't know which half."

Then the web came along and, like magic, advertising wasn't limited by space and time. Once online, your brochure could be a hundred pages, but printing and postage wouldn't cost you a penny. So, the web became another channel to push out those ads. "Brochureware" websites were born and the sales copy was simply pasted in from other advertisements. Little, if any, effort was made to treat the web as a unique channel with new opportunities.

But unlike traditional marketing, web traffic was measurable. People began to talk about how many "hits" their online brochures were getting.

Then, a shift...

Slow, steady changes in technology and consumer behavior reached a tipping point. Suddenly the website was the center of all marketing efforts. The push of the traditional ad campaigns directed consumers to the web. Every billboard, TV commercial, radio spot and magazine insert had a web address at the bottom.

As people began to see the value of web marketing, billions in marketing budgets were moved toward search engine optimization, pay-per-click advertising and email marketing.

Also during this time, traditional advertising became less effective. Consumers had more ways than ever to dodge the interruptions of advertising. Spam filters blocked unwelcome email. DVRs skipped distracting TV ads. Banner blockers cleaned the blinking boxes off websites. "Do not call" lists helped keep the telemarketers away.

Welcome to modern marketing! It's new and improved, with more creative ways to connect with the people who matter to you. And the best part is that if you create meaningful content, those people will come to you.

The barriers have been removed and, rather than advertise on television, you can be your own TV station. Rather than seek publicity through PR, you can start your own online newsroom and grow your readership. You'll spend less money on printing and postage, and more time teaching something useful. You are on the web, and the web is in people's pockets.

We are in a golden era of social, video and mobile marketing, and it's built on content. The simple act of reading this book means you are likely to take advantage of these combined mega-trends.

Ready? Let's go.

Content Marketing vs. Advertising

Content marketing (also known as inbound marketing) is nothing new. It is simply using content to connect with potential buyers and partners. The content earns the interest and trust of the audience by being entertaining or informative.

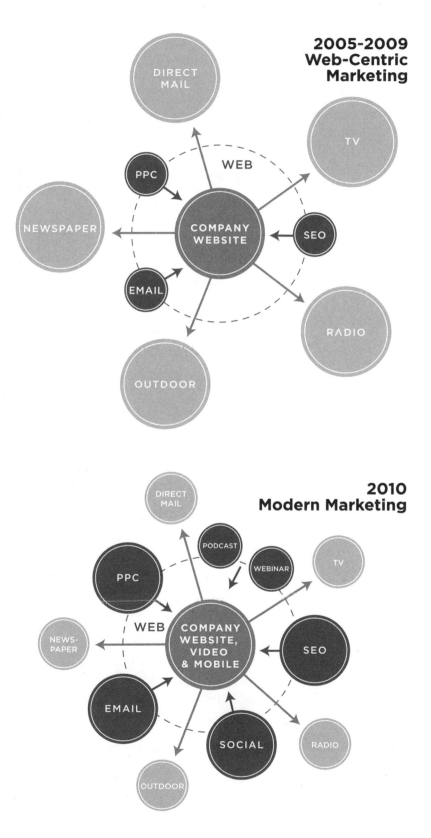

Content marketing is not only different from advertising, it's the opposite of it. Content marketers attract their audience by being relevant. Advertisers inject themselves into other relevant media, hoping to be noticed. It's pull versus push.

Content Marketing (inbound)	Advertising (outbound)
Teach, help	Sell
Attract, interact, connect	Distract, interrupt
Brains	Budgets
The magnet	The hammer

In the words of Jay Baer, content is the **help**. Advertising is the **hype**.

You're probably like me.

You probably don't like to be interrupted by TV or magazine ads. You probably don't click on many banner ads. You probably use a spam filter.

You probably like to look for things on your own terms, research the options and read reviews. You probably listen to input from friends and you may even share recommendations with them.

This explains why content marketing is emerging as a winner. It's a friendlier, more credible and more sensitive way for us to connect with information, including the information that drives our purchasing decisions. Dollar-for-dollar and hour-for-hour, inbound is beating outbound.

Let's start by looking at how websites make money...

Web Strategy and Website ROI

Whether you're spending cash out-of-pocket or just investing your time, the return on investment in web marketing comes down to three main factors:

- Traffic (number of visitors)
- Conversion rate (percentage of visitors taking action, becoming leads or subscribers, etc.)
- Maintenance costs

That's it! Generally speaking, traffic times the conversion rate equals leads. Subtract from that the time and cost of managing and promoting the site, and you have your ROI. Simple, right?

Everything a content chemist does should increase traffic and conversions while minimizing the cost and time in any way possible.

Going one level deeper, we can see how the variables are determined. Let's look at a fictional case study and show how ROI can be calculated. This example will be an imaginary business that seeks to generate leads from visitors who find the site through search engines.

Case Study: Libby's Laboratory Services

Like a lot of businesses, Libby's business provides a service that people look for online.

Libby offers laboratory services, including staffing and testing, to research facilities. She's been doing this for a while and she's good at it. But Libby needs more leads if she's going to grow her business, and it's hard to connect with researchers looking for lab services.

So how much money will Libby make from her website and content marketing? How much new business will she get? How many leads would the site need to generate in order to pay for itself? What is the return on this investment? Let's figure it out.

Traffic...

Well, Libby won't have any leads if she doesn't get any traffic. She has a relatively unknown brand. She's in a small niche and wants search engines to help people find her business.

To estimate search engine traffic, she'll need to investigate the "search volume" of her top keyphrases. She needs to know how many monthly searches there are for "laboratory staffing." If the new site ranks high for these phrases, people will see Libby's site in the search engine listings.

Each time the site appears in a search results page is an "impression." Of course, the more phrases Libby's site ranks for, the more impressions she'll get. So she'll want to target a range of phrases.

But how high she ranks is also a big factor. A higher rank means exponentially more clicks (see *fig. 2c*). All other things being equal, the top ranking site gets a LOT more traffic than number two, and so on down the line. The effect of rank on traffic is exponential, so Libby plans to target some phrases that aren't too competitive.

Two factors determine the total number of impressions: *the number of keyphrases a site ranks for and the rank for each keyphrase.* Therefore...

$$(\text{Number of Keyphrases})(\text{Search Volume}^{\text{Rank}}) = \text{Impressions}$$

⚠️ **WARNING!** This formula is for illustrative purposes only. Here, a higher rank in search engines would mean a larger "rank" number in the formula. Also, in reality, search volume and rank are per keyphrase, and not simply multiplied by the number of keyphrases. Unlike the other formulas in this book, you can't simply plug numbers into this one!

When the site ranks, it attracts an audience and some of them will click. The percentage of searchers that click on Libby's listing is the "clickthrough rate" or CTR. Each click is a visit.

$$\text{Impressions} \times \text{CTR} = \text{Visits}$$

So the more phrases, the higher the rank, the more popular the phrases, the more impressions and ultimately, more visits. Sound complicated?

Fortunately for Libby, her cousin Dale is a web strategist. Together, they research keyphrases and check search volume in Wordtracker and Google Adwords (see Chapter 4 for details). They check the competition using Google, OpenSiteExplorer and Alexa. Then they estimate clickthrough rates by looking at similar sites in Google Analytics and Google

Webmaster Tools. They make an educated guess and estimate that with a well-optimized site *they can eventually expect 1,000 targeted visitors per month from search engines.*

...times conversions...

Getting traffic from search engines is great, but it's not the same as leads. If a researcher looking for lab services finds Libby's website, he's not a lead yet. He's just a visitor. When a lead calls or fills out Libby's contact form, he is officially a "conversion." The better the site, the higher the "conversion rate." There are many factors that determine the conversion rate, including design quality (brand loyalty and overall appeal), content format (text, images and video), the content itself (compelling, informative and relevant) and usability (navigation and an easy-to-use form).

Visits x Conversion Rate = Leads

Libby meets with Dale again to do more research. They study industry benchmarks and look at other laboratory services sites. They assume Libby's new site will be excellent—or at least good—in all of the conversion factors listed above. In the end, *they figure a 2% conversion rate is attainable.* Thanks again, Dale!

...equals leads...

Now all they have to do is multiply the projected visits by the estimated conversion rate. They calculate that *the site should generate 20 leads per month.*

...times closing rate...

Now they need to convert the leads into actual customers. Dale can't help here, but Libby has a pretty good sales process in place and she can close around 50% of her leads. Each time she does this, she sells $1,000 worth of lab services. It costs her about $500 in time and overhead each time she provides this service. So generally speaking, the value of a lead to Libby is about $500.

Now that we have all the pieces, we can put them together in a (very cumbersome but comprehensive) set of formulas for estimating the return on the investment for a marketing website.*

(Leads x Closing Rate)(Price-Time and Materials) = Profit

$$K \times (S^R) = I$$
$$I \times CTR = V$$
$$V \times CR = L$$
$$(L \times CL)(P - Dc) = \$$$

K = number of kephrases
S = search volume
R = rank
V = visits
L = leads
P = price
$ = profit!

CTR = clickthrough rate (search engines)
CR = conversion rate (website)
CL = closing rate (sales)
Dc = delivery costs or cost of goods and services sold (time and materials)

*There are other many other variables that could have been incorporated into this formula (including other sources of traffic, etc.) but to add them all here would have made the forumula more confusing than useful.

...equals profit.

Now it's time to do the math. Let's plug in Libby's estimates.

(20 leads x 0.5 closing rate)
($1,000 lab service price - $500
time & materials)=$5,000 profit

If Libby can meet all of the targets above, *her website and marketing efforts will bring in up to $5,000 in profitable leads per month. In other words, if she invests $15,000 and ranks well and converts visitors, the website will pay for itself in 3 months. After that, it will be profitable.* Over its lifetime, the new site will likely generate tens of thousands of visitors, thousands of leads and hundreds of thousands of dollars in revenue and profit.

But Libby isn't expecting instant results. She knows something very important...

A great site is not enough

Libby knows that launching the site is just the beginning. There is still is a lot of work to do, but she's committed to content marketing.

- She's going to do the ongoing work to get results in search engines. She knows that search engine marketing takes time.

- She's going to consistently create and promote relevant content.

- She's going to boost traffic with a new email newsletter called *Laboratory Services Monthly*.

- She's committed to following up on her web leads and tracking them using a database like Highrise or SalesForce.

And most of all, Libby is committed to providing the best possible laboratory services. She plans to have a visible presence and a good reputation, both online and off.

Getting traffic from
search engines is great,
but it's not the same as leads.

What You'll Need

Now you should have a sense of what content marketing really is and how it differs from advertising. We saw how marketing has evolved and where the big-picture trends are going. And we looked briefly at the end results and how they're measured.

To take advantage of the techniques in this book, you'll need a website. You'll also need tools to go along with it. Here are the basic tools for content marketing:

1. Blog: The blog should share the same domain as your main website, so the address of the blog is http://blog.website.com or http://www.website.com/blog (preferably the latter).

If you do not have a blog, you will still be able to use many of these techniques with web pages rather than blog posts, assuming you can easily update your website using a Content Management System (CMS) such as WordPress, Mighty-Site or Drupal.

If you do not have a blog, you will still be able to use many of these techniques with web pages rather than blog posts, assuming you can easily update your website using a Content Management System (CMS) such as WordPress, Mighty-Site or Drupal.

2. Contact Form for Lead Generation: A contact page with an email link is insufficient, since it will not allow you to easily measure results. If your business sells products on an ecommerce site, the shopping cart will be more important than this contact form.

3. Email Service Provider (ESP): ESPs such as MailChimp, Constant Contact and Express Pigeon provide email marketing templates and service for sending mass emails, and offer reporting tools.

4. Web Analytics: Google Analytics or Hubspot is necessary for measuring activity on the website. Without measurement, there is no data to inform iterative improvements.

5. Social Media Presence: For the more advanced techniques found in this book, you will need a basic presence in the social networks. This generally means thoughtful, complete profiles on Twitter, Google+, LinkedIn and/or Facebook, with enough activity and followers to make you and your business look credible.

If you have these tools, and the motivation to embrace content marketing principles, you're ready to go.

PART ONE:
LECTURE

How it all Works

There are a lot of factors that contribute to the success of websites and web marketing. Let's start by take a giant step back and look at all the things required to win attention, generate demand and drive leads and sales.

Here is our all-in-one, super huge, print-this-and-hang-it-up explanation of everything you need to know about how website and web marketing combine to get results. *(fig 1)* You'll see there are many little things that add up to the final outcome. In the Lab section, you'll find detailed instructions for the tactics mentioned here. **Do not skip any steps**. Miss something here and you'll miss opportunities to connect with customers.

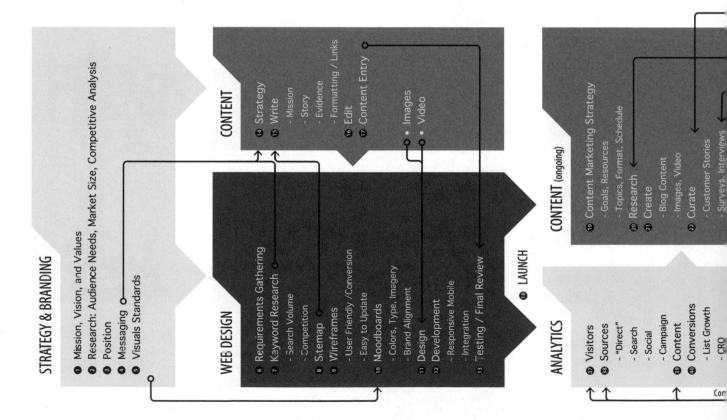

STRATEGY & BRANDING

❶ Mission, Vision, and Values
❷ Research: Audience Needs, Market Size, Competitive Analysis
❸ Position
❹ Messaging
❺ Visuals Standards

CONTENT

⓮ Strategy
⓯ Write
  - Mission
  - Story
  - Evidence
  - Formatting / Links
⓰ Edit
⓱ Content Entry
  • Images
  • Video

WEB DESIGN

❻ Requirements Gathering
❼ Keyword Research
  - Search Volume
  - Competition
❽ Sitemap
❾ Wireframes
  - User Friendly /Conversion
  - Easy to Update
❿ Moodboards
  - Colors, Type, Imagery
  - Brand Alignment
⓫ Design
⓬ Development
  - Responsive Mobile
  - Integration
⓭ Testing / Final Review

⓲ LAUNCH

CONTENT (ongoing)

⓳ Content Marketing Strategy
  - Goals: Resources
  - Topics, Format, Schedule
⓴ Research
㉑ Create
  - Blog Content
  - Images, Video
㉒ Curate
  - Customer Stories
  - Surveys, Interviews

ANALYTICS

㊲ Visitors
㊳ Sources
  - "Direct"
  - Search
  - Social
  - Campaign
㊴ Content
㊵ Conversions
  - List Growth
  - CRO

Strategy

It all starts with a clear understanding of why you're in business and how you deliver value to your customers.

1. Mission, Vision and Values:
Why are you in business? What is your core offering? What does your company stand for? Know these first or you're building your marketing on sand.

2. Research: Audience Needs, Market Size, Competitive Analysis:
Know your niche. How do you meet the demands of your audience? What is your place in the market? Are you up against big, consolidated competitors? Or are you in a fragmented market? *Content strategy is the bait to use, but audience strategy is the pond to fish in.*

Branding

Now you can create the perception you will project into the market. Branding is the perception of your position in the market, including all your content and imagery. It should be consistent from the first impression throughout the entire experience of each of your visitors and customers.

3. Position:
Now you can get specific about your target audience and their unmet needs. What is your unique point of difference? Use a positioning template to guide you through the positioning thought process.

My good friend Susan Silver of Argentum Strategy recommends using this simple one to guide your thinking.

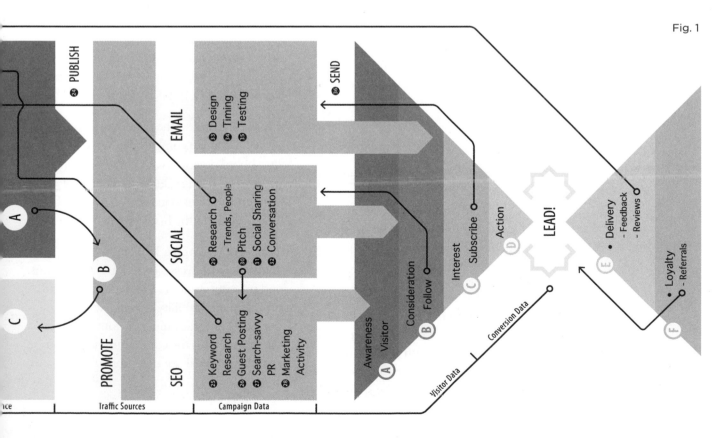

Fig. 1

To (target audience) with (unmet need), (company name) is the (competitive set) that (unique point of difference) because it (evidence 1, 2, 3) .

If you can't fill in all five of these using only a few words, sharpen your focus on this step before proceeding.

4. **Messaging**: How best to describe the value you provide? What evidence do you have to support your unique point of difference? Align your message with your position and your values. Find a clear and concise voice.

5. **Visual Standards:** Create a visual continuity through colors, styles and type. Carry this through your website, your offline materials, your social networks, your email marketing and each piece of your content.

Web Design

The website is both the platform for publishing and the machine for generating leads. A great site pulls in traffic like a magnet, builds trust and gives valuable information to visitors. It's also easy to update and connects with other systems.

6. **Gathering Requirements**: Step one in a great site is knowing what the scope will be. What features need to be included? What kinds of changes may be needed down the road? How many types of page templates will there be?

7. **Keyword Research**: People are looking for you right now. If you find out what they're searching for, you can align pages on the website with phrases that they're searching for. Make sure to research keywords before you make the sitemap.

8. **Sitemap:** The organization of the pages determines how the site will be navigated by visitors. What information do visitors need, and in what order, before they become a lead? The sitemap also affects how search-friendly the pages are. What page labels best indicate your relevance? Ideally, you create your sitemap with both visitors and search engines in mind.

9. **Wireframes:** The wireframes are the black-and-white layouts for the page templates. Like the sitemap, wireframes have several purposes. They function as a planning tool for the user experience. But these layouts also affect search-friendliness and ease of updates. This is also where responsive web design and mobile-friendliness is planned. One template is created for each type of page.

10. **Moodboards**: If the wireframes are about structure, the moodboards are about style. Here's where the visual standards are executed online. Background colors, button styles and type treatments are set for headers, links and body text.

11. **Design**: Next the wireframes and moodboards are combined into the storyboard designs. Now all the planning comes to life. The visual prominence of each element is balanced in relation to the others as usability and the brand come together.

12. **Development**: Final designs are converted into web pages first through front-end programming: HTML and CSS, and browser compatibility testing. Next comes back-end programming: custom features, integration into the content management system and database development.

13. Testing and Final Review: Everything must be double-checked to ensure it works properly on all browsers in all devices. Pages must load quickly and each feature must be bug-free.

Website Content

The website content is created during the web design process. Once the sitemap is final, the full scope of the content requirements is set. The initial content for the main marketing pages should be finalized before development is complete, or the launch will be delayed.

14. Strategy: What questions does your audience have? What concerns? What do they desire, fear, trust and love? The website content must be aligned with the people who will be reading it. Create personas if necessary. Align the topics and tone with the audience.

15. Write: Write with these readers in mind. Respect the time of the readers and be concise. Think ahead about traffic and use the target phrases. Pay close attention to formatting and internal linking. Select images and create videos that build credibility. Put your best foot forward, but be humble.

16. Edit: Make sure the content is accurate and on-target, but don't delay the launch while you wordsmith that paragraph for two weeks. Web content is easy, free and fast to change any time.

17. Content Entry: All final content is added to the content management system, including images, videos, metadata and page titles. All formatting, including headers, bullets and links, is checked one last time.

18. LAUNCH!: The big day. For most businesses, it comes just once every four to five years. Hopefully, the design, programming and content are all ready to go. But again, don't let small issues delay the launch. Digital ink is never dry. You can (and should) change the site as time goes by.

Now the platform is in place and we're ready to start content marketing.

Create Content

A website without a steady stream of useful content is just an online brochure. It has no pulse. It is simply an online advertisement. But add useful content and suddenly, there's a bigger reason to visit. There's a reason to share, to link and to open the newsletters. Content generates the trust that generates the fans, the leads and the sales.

> A website without a steady stream of useful content is just an online brochure. **It has no pulse.**

19. Content Marketing Strategy: A *sustainable* content marketing plan is based on the resources available: people, money and time, both internally and from vendors and partners. An *effective* content marketing plan is based on topics, tone and frequency that align with the needs of the audience. Personas and publishing calendars will help.

20. Research: A carefully researched article is more useful to your audience than an opinion piece. Thorough "how-to" posts are more likely to be searched for, shared, bookmarked and read. Do your research and create something valuable. Surveys and original research with evidence are among the highest-value content on the web.

> Do your research and **create something valuable**. Surveys and original research with evidence are among the highest-value content on the web.

21. Create: Write the posts, record the podcasts or shoot the videos—whichever *format* is best for your audience. Use a ghostwriter, content template, content checklist or restaurant napkin—whichever *method* is best for you and your team.

22. Curate: Repurpose content from other sources, but add your own insights and perspective. Interviews, event recaps and article round-ups are all efficient ways to produce high-value content quickly.

23. Edit: Your process should include an editorial review to make sure you don't publish typos and mistakes. Simple errors can hurt credibility and make you look foolish. Take the time to have an editor review the work.

24. PUBLISH!: Make it live. For posts, publish using a URL that includes the target keyphrase. For videos, embed them into your site using a professional hosting service.

Content Promotion

Now we're ready to promote our content. It's not enough to just publish. Our focus here is content marketing, not advertising. That means making your content visible through search engine optimization, social media and email marketing. It's time to market your marketing.

Search Engine Optimization

Ranking in search engines can provide a durable, consistent source of traffic. It requires research, careful writing and a credible website and domain. This means enough link popularity to compete for the phrases you're targeting.

25. Keyword Research: As with web page content, blog posts and other content marketing should be aligned with keyphrases. As before, select keyphrases based on search volume, competition and relevance. You'll use these keyphrases in your writing using SEO best practices outlined in Chapter 3.

26. Guest Blogging: Your content shouldn't be limited to your own site. Writing high-quality content and submitting it to relevant blogs is good for branding and SEO. It's a way to put your message in front of a new audience and make new friends.

27. Search-savvy PR: Public relations activity can also create great linking opportunities. PR professionals who know the value of links take advantage of any media attention to seek authoritative links to specific web pages and blog posts.

28. Other Marketing Activity: Of course, this goes beyond search optimization, but it's worth noting that all kinds of offline marketing have potential search benefits. Events, partnerships, advertising, association memberships and sponsorships can all create link opportunities.

Social Media

Social media marketing is a powerful channel for promoting content and an indespensible tool for online networking. Both of these outcomes are important for lead generation. Great social media includes content promotion, content curation and one-to-one conversation.

29. Research: Find specific people to connect with, such as prospects, bloggers, journalists, editors and influencers. Build lists of people to watch. Carefully research publications and blogs before pitching content.

30. Pitch: For both PR and guest blogging, pitching content goes hand-in-hand with social media. Use social channels to gradually build stronger connections. Submit content with humility and sensitivity to the audience of the blog or publication. Always be thoughtful of editors' time.

31. Social Sharing: Post your content on the social networks where your audience spends time. Don't be shy. Believe in your content and share each post multiple times over days, weeks and months. Deliberately share the post with people who will love what you wrote on social media and even with personal emails.

32. Conversation: Don't let your social stream fill up with promotional posts. Talk to people! Use social media as a tool for networking. When possible, move the conversation from casual mentions on Twitter to email, phone and face-to-face meetings.

Email Marketing

Search engines and social networks are all owned by companies—but your email list belongs to you and your business. An engaged list of subscribers who look forward to your content is one of the most powerful tools for nurturing and generating leads.

33. Design and Production: Your email template should be lightweight, mobile-friendly and easy to manage. Your subject line should be descriptive but leave room for curiosity. Your teaser text and call to action should be crafted to maximize clickthroughs.

34. Timing and Frequency: When is your audience most likely to open? Friday at lunch or Saturday morning? How often should you send email? If your sales cycle is long, you may only need to send something monthly. Focus on quality, not quantity. Grow your audience by politely inviting your current prospects to join your list.

35. Testing: Email marketing is easy to track, so each email is an opportunity for measurement and improvement. Use A/B test subject lines and experiment with timing. Add tracking codes using the Google URL Builder to compare campaigns. Keep experimenting and improving.

36. SEND!: Send emails using a professional service with good deliverability (99%) and easy-to-read reports. Keep your list clean by checking bounces and removing old addresses.

> The two most important numbers for lead generation are **total traffic and the conversion rate**. All efforts are focused on these two numbers.

Analytics

Analytics is a decision support tool. Use it to do real analysis and check the results of experiments. The two most important numbers for lead generation are total traffic and conversion rate. All efforts are focused on these two numbers.

37. Visitors and Overall Traffic Levels: Adjusting for seasonality, is traffic up or down? Is your content attracting more visitors over time? Are the visitors bouncing after one page or going deeper into your website?

38. Traffic Sources: Where are visitors coming from? Which of your promotion channels are effective? Which keyphrases, email campaigns and social channels are pulling in visitors?

39. Content Performance: Which pages are connecting with visitors? Which topics are getting traction? Which are most successful at generating traffic and conversions?

40. Conversions: The bottom line is the total number of leads or ecommerce sales. The **total traffic** times your **conversion rate** equals success. Other conversions include newsletter subscribers, job applicants and event registrants. Social follows are also conversions, but they don't appear in Analytics

Now let's start at the top and take a look at the different sources of website traffic.

Traffic Sources

When you look at your website analytics (Google Analytics, Hubspot, etc.) you'll see that traffic is generally categorized into three groups:

- **Search traffic** - visitors who found you by searching for a keyphrase in a search engine
- **Referring traffic** - visitors who clicked a link on a website and landed at your site
- **Direct traffic** - visitors who typed your web address into their browser

Although it's interesting, this breakdown of traffic is not all that accurate or meaningful. For example, you might think search traffic is new people who found you out of the blue. But some of that traffic is likely old friends who searched for your business name, so that number is often misleading.

Although direct traffic is supposedly from visitors who typed the address into a browser or clicked on a bookmark, it actually includes many other types of traffic. Any visits that are not from referring websites or search engines are lumped into direct traffic. This includes visitors who clicked on links that weren't in browsers, such as links in Twitter apps and email programs. Not all direct traffic is truly direct.

Here's an example. Suppose you send an email newsletter to two subscribers. One uses Outlook and the other uses Yahoo! mail. Since Outlook is installed software and Yahoo! mail is used in a web browser, the subscriber who clicks from Outlook will be recorded as direct traffic. The other, who clicked from within a browser while using Yahoo!, may be recorded as referring traffic. In fact, both visitors came from an email campaign, which isn't really what direct or referring traffic is supposed to be. More about tracking email traffic soon.

There are advanced ways to set up Google Analytics to minimize these tracking issues. But first, let's focus on driving results rather than tweaking how results are measured.

As a content marketer, you must plan to generate traffic *through activity*. Let's re-categorize the traffic sources to align them with our three main content marketing techniques: Search Engine Marketing, Social Media and Email Marketing.

Search Engine Optimization (SEO)

Search engines are a critical source of traffic for almost every site. Watch your own behavior online for a few hours and you'll find yourself entering keyphrases and searching Google or one of the other search engines.

Since two-thirds of all searches happen within Google, we'll focus there. But the principles of ranking in Google are fundamentally similar across all search engines.

Ultimately, all SEO efforts have one focus: to indicate that your site is relevant. Every time you see or hear the phrase "search engine optimization," substitute the words "indicating relevance" and you'll have the right mindset for good SEO work.

Your goal is simply to help Google help people find you. Cooperate with Google and stay on their good side. The key to SEO is to have valuable content and confirm this to Google with great links from relevant sites.

The outcomes of successful SEO efforts can be impressive: (*Fig. 2a*)

As a site gradually ranks higher and ranks for a wider range of phrases, traffic climbs. (*Fig. 2b*)

Fig. 2a

Fig. 2b

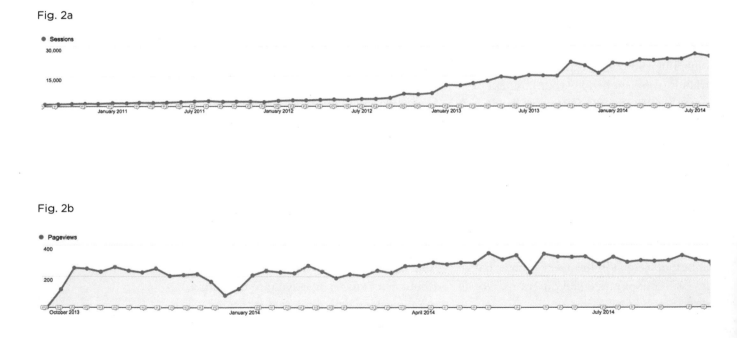

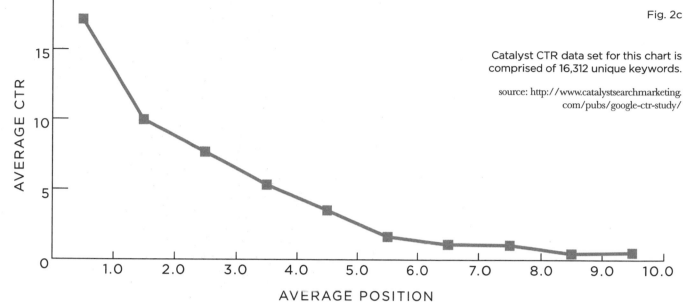

2013 Catalyst

Fig. 2c

Catalyst CTR data set for this chart is comprised of 16,312 unique keywords.

source: http://www.catalystsearchmarketing.com/pubs/google-ctr-study/

An individual post may be initially promoted through email, but if it also ranks well in search engines it will continue to get traffic for years.

Ranking high in search engine results is exponentially better than ranking low. Potential visitors tend to trust that Google delivers relevant results, so the top-ranking sites get a disproportionate share of the glory.

According to search marketing company Catalyst, the first three spots in Google get 35% of all clicks. The top spot gets 17%, second place gets 10% and so on down the line. Everyone knows that page two is no-man's land, but not everyone realizes that ranking first drives almost five times as much traffic as ranking fifth. Here's the data. (*Fig. 2c*)

WARNING! *Black Hat vs. White Hat SEO:* Some search optimizers try to trick Google by using techniques that go beyond indicating relevance. They stuff pages full of keyphrases, hide keyphrases behind images or use the same color for text and backgrounds. Some even program their websites to show different versions of content depending on whether the visitor is Google or human. They also buy, rent and trade with people to get more links to their sites.

These are all considered "Black Hat" techniques; they can be destructive and are not recommended. Remember, Google has a small army of math PhDs led by Matt Cutts, Google's head of web spam. These people are smarter than you and me. If they catch you using Black Hat tricks, they have every right to put you on their blacklist.

Once blacklisted, your domain will never rank again, even when people search for the business name. This is a devastating outcome for a content marketer.

Stick to the usual "White Hat" techniques and focus on indicating your relevance. Provide valuable content that is focused on topics (keyphrases) relevant to your audience. Build genuine connections (links) with relevant websites.

NOTE! Search engine marketing is typically a slow, long-term form of marketing. It can take years of work to rank for an important phrase. It's called "optimization" because it's an iterative, ongoing process. SEO is evolutionary, not revolutionary. Be patient.

Why do Sites Rank in Search Engines?

This is an important question. Google's secret formula is far more valuable than the recipe for Coke. Although we'll never know for sure what the algorithm is, there are thousands of people researching it every day. They work tirelessly to better understand the criteria Google uses to determine who ranks for which phrases.

NOTE! Google offers their own SEO advice on the Official *Webmaster Central Blog*. It encourages website owners to provide valuable content. Solid advice.

One of my favorite search engine research companies is Moz. Every two years, they send a survey to some of the top search engine optimizers around the world. The results are published as the Search Ranking Factors and may be one of the best publicly available sources of information about how Google works.

The Moz 2013 Search Ranking Factors surveyed 120 optimizers, and the aggregate of their expert opinions looks like this: (*Fig 3a*)

To avoid going into the technical details of things like "page level keyword agnostic features," I'm simplifying this chart by breaking down these factors into five groups and redrawing the chart as follows: (*Fig 3b*)

Link popularity: Links from other websites to your website.

On-page SEO: Attributes of your website, such as the use of keywords on your pages.

Domain name: This includes use of keywords in your domain.

Social activity: This includes sharing on Facebook and Twitter.

Other: This includes factors such as content freshness, the number of searches for the company name, the time it takes pages to load, the number of errors, clickthrough rates from search engines, etc.

Suddenly it's clear that links on other people's websites are a big factor in how high you rank in search engines. If you're serious about SEO, getting good links has to be part of your content marketing efforts (more about link building in Chapter 4).

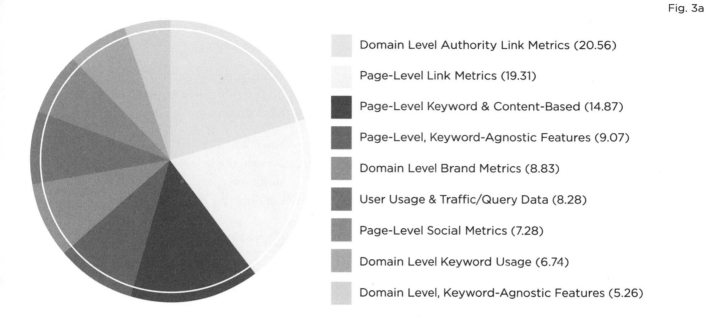

Fig. 3a

Domain Level Authority Link Metrics (20.56)

Page-Level Link Metrics (19.31)

Page-Level Keyword & Content-Based (14.87)

Page-Level, Keyword-Agnostic Features (9.07)

Domain Level Brand Metrics (8.83)

User Usage & Traffic/Query Data (8.28)

Page-Level Social Metrics (7.28)

Domain Level Keyword Usage (6.74)

Domain Level, Keyword-Agnostic Features (5.26)

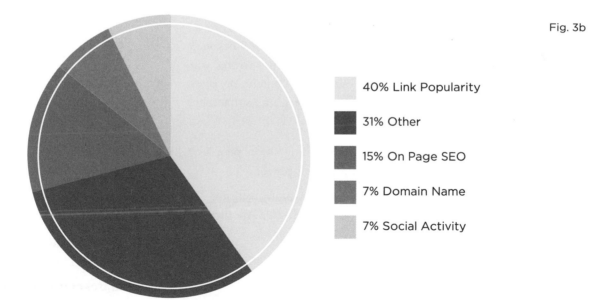

Fig. 3b

40% Link Popularity

31% Other

15% On Page SEO

7% Domain Name

7% Social Activity

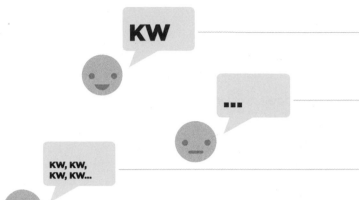

Now that we have a general idea of how search engines work, let's introduce the three key SEO-related activities that a content marketer should focus on:

- Keyphrase research
- On-page search optimization
- Link popularity

Keyphrase Research

The first step in search marketing is always the same: picking your keyphrases. If you do everything else right but get this wrong, you won't see any results. As a content marketer, you must carefully choose phrases that meet three criteria:

- **Search volume**: How many people are searching for this phrase?

- **Competition**: How many websites are relevant for this phrase? Are they powerful sites?

- **Relevance**: If someone found your site while searching for this phrase, would they be happy? Would you be happy they found you?

The goal is to align the page with a relevant phrase. The ideal keyphrase has high volume, low competition and is highly relevant to your business. Specific techniques for researching keyphrases are found in Chapter 3.

Choose a keyword for which people are really searching and that is relevant to your topic.

You're unlikely to rank if you don't deliberately target a phrase. SEO doesn't happen by accident!

You could also hurt your rankings if you overuse the keyword on the page. Keyword stuffing is spam. Indicate relevance, but don't try too hard.

On-Page SEO

There are many ways to indicate on your pages that your content is relevant. As a writer of web content, you have multiple opportunities to indicate your pages' relevance for the target keyphrase. It often requires some small compromises to the writing, but if done well the page will rank much higher and be seen by many more people. It's worth the compromise. Trust me.

Here's a list of the most important places to use your target phrase to help Google understand that you are relevant. They are listed in order of importance.

- **Title**: Between <title> and </title>.
- **Headers**: Between <h1> and </h1> as well as <h2> and so on.
- **Body text**: This is all the text on the page that isn't within links.
- **Meta description**: Although it doesn't actually appear on the web page, the meta description often appears in search results as the snippet.

Chapter 4 has more detail on the specific ways you should use keyphrases in your writing.

Links

Google considers more than 200 factors when ranking websites, but none are more important than links. When many websites link to a page, that page is more likely to rank in search engines. Link popularity still matters. A lot.

Think about it: if 1,000 websites link to a page about the U-505 submarine and each of those 1,000 links have text such as "learn more about the U-505 submarine," then the page must be relevant for that topic. The links are a powerful indicator of relevance. This is especially true if those 1,000 sites are also about submarines and those sites have many inbound links themselves.

This is why link popularity is an excellent way for search engines to see what sites are really about. As we saw from the Moz research above, link popularity is a heavily weighted ranking factor. Why? Because it's hard to fake. If SEO was only about which page uses the phrase most often, anyone could put "U-505 submarine" on the page a hundred times and rank high. Google would then be full of spam. This is why links matter so much.

So, link text (also known as anchor text) is very important. If you're hoping to rank for "kids' jet packs," then it's a good thing if there are some links to your site with this phrase in the link text.

> ...link popularity is a heavily weighted ranking factor. Why? Because **it's hard to fake**.

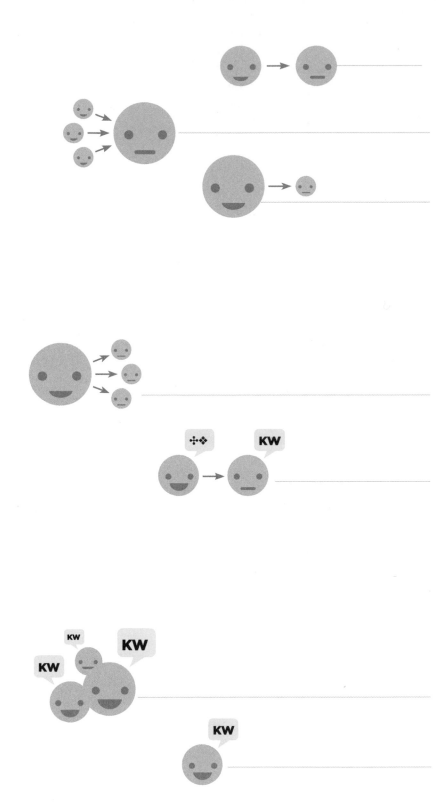

When a another website links to one of your pages, it's a vote of confidence. It's an indication of relevance, and Google notices.

When many sites link to one of your web pages, even better. Link popularity works like any popularity contest. You want a lot of votes.

The best links are from sites that have a high link popularity themselves. These links are worth more. Just like a popularity contest, one vote from someone popular is worth more than a dozen votes from the unknown.

If a page is linking to several sites, the value of those links is divided. So a link to you from a page that's also linking to all kinds of other pages isn't as valuable.

Again, in a popularity contest, if the person who votes for you is voting for three people at once, it's not as good. You're really only getting a third of a vote.

Links from related sites are generally better. A link from a completely irrelevant site is not as valuable, since that site doesn't have as much credibility on that topic.

Competition and Keywords

Now that you understand link popularity, consider your target keyword. The likelihood of ranking for that phrase depends on the competition.

Do the high-ranking sites for the keyword have higher link popularity than you? Then choose another keyword.

If your link popularity is low, start with a narrow niche and target longer, more specific keywords. It's better to rank first for a less popular phrase than rank on page 50 for a big-money keyword.

Link Text: The Words within Those Links

The link text (or anchor text) is the word or words that make up the link. The link text for this link is "this link." Make sense?

Lots of times, link text is simply "click here" or "www.example.com." But when link text includes a keyword, it can be another indication of relevance. If the links to a page say "flying carpet safety," then Google is likely to believe that this is what the page is about.

It's good to have links that include the target keyword.

When too many links to a page include the target keyword, it may look spammy. Google may penalize you for "over-optimization."

Don't try too hard to get links with your exact keyword as link text. It looks unnatural. Balance is good.

Follow vs. nofollow: As Google crawls the zillions of pages of the Internet, it follows links from one site to the next. Commenting on blogs often creates a link back to the website of the commenter. When SEOs realized they could generate links just by commenting, blogs were flooded with low value comments. Website owners can tell Google not to follow certain links by adding a tiny code that says "nofollow." Google skips these links, which then have much less value (if any) to

the website on the other end. Today, most popular blogs have links within comments set to "nofollow," so blog commenting is not considered an important SEO tactic.

When you're looking at websites as possible linking opportunities, it's important to make sure that the link isn't designated "nofollow." It would be frustrating to spend hours writing and editing a high-quality guest blog post, give it to a relevant site, see it go live…and then realize that the link to your site is tagged "nofollow" (more on guest blogging in Chapter 5).

⚠️ **WARNING!** Some links may actually hurt your rankings. Anything that looks spammy or unnatural is bad. For example, if suddenly there are 500 new links to your site from low-quality pages with irrelevant content, Google may see this as "link farming" and you may be penalized. Similarly, Google may notice if lots of your links are from sites that you link back to. This type of "reciprocal linking" may also get flagged as possible spam.

Don't try too hard to get links with your exact keyword as link text. It looks unnatural. **Balance is good.**

The Two Types of Visitors Who Come From Search Engines

When it all works, your website will attract two distinct types of visitors. They are searching using two very different types of phrases.

QUESTIONS

Looking for answers

Searchers researching problems

Don't yet know what they need

 QUESTION MARKS

ANSWERS

Looking for a presumed solution

Know what they want

Ready to make a decision/buy

 DOLLAR SIGNS

They are finding two different types of content on your website.

BLOG POSTS & ARTICLES

USUALLY:

Detailed, how-to posts

Lists

Educational

Lots of text

Competes with content providers

PRODUCT & SERVICE PAGES

USUALLY:

Pages that sell

Includes evidence & CTA's

Stories

Address objections

Competes with business

They look very different from each other within your Analytics.

LONG, ONE-PAGE VISITS

High bounce rate

Few pages per session

High % of new users

SHORT TIME PER PAGE, MANY PAGES PER VISIT

Lower bounce rate

Lower time on page

Higher coversion rate, page value

And they support two different parts of your marketing funnel.

Understanding that search engines attract these two very different types of visitors will help you understand what effects your content has on your Analytics.

SEO Summary

In the end, ranking in search engines and indicating your relevance comes down to great content written by a credible author and supported by great links. In other words, if you want to rank high, be good. Build and maintain a great online presence. If you are the best site on the Internet for that topic, Google will try hard to help people find you.

Target good keyphrases, use them in appropriate ways and look for opportunities to get high-quality links to your site. But above all, *strive to be truly relevant.*

In the Lab section, you'll learn the specific techniques for researching keyphrases.

Social Media Marketing

Traffic from social media is the direct result of activity. Unlike traffic from search engines, where one page may rank well for years, messages within social media tend to be short-lived because the stream of posts and Tweets flows on with time. If you're active in social channels and you stop, so does the traffic. *(fig. 4a)*

The good news is that by being active in social channels you can drive traffic relatively quickly, especially if your social network is already developed. If you post or Tweet today, you'll get traffic today.

Social media is a skill like anything else. An expert knows ways to dramatically increase the odds of good things happening. A novice or someone who understands social media but not marketing is not as likely to drive results. Well, they might drive somewhere, but not toward a measurable goal.

A developed social media network is an important tool for every content marketer. Here is a quick list of specific benefits of using social networks:

- Find and connect with people who are likely to share your content

- Thank people who have helped you

- Increase your chances of getting press, speaking engagements and guest blogging opportunities by offering to help with promotion

- Monitor trends by following experts

- Test out possible email subject lines

- Promote your content and the content of others in your network

Increase your chances of getting press, speaking engagements and guest blogging opportunities by offering to **help with promotion.**

Fig. 4a

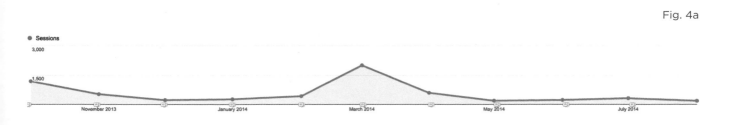

Sessions
3,000

1,500

November 2013   January 2014   March 2014   May 2014   July 2014

Fig. 4b

(adapted from
Hutch Carpenter's
"Is Google+ More
Facebook or More
Twitter? Yes." and
Guy Kowasaki's Why
I Love Google+.
LinkedIn column
added by author)

Facebook	Google+	Twitter	LinkedIn
Two-way connecting	One-way following	One-way following	Two-way connecting
Friends lists	Circles for tracking	Lists	
Groups	Circles for limited sharing		Groups
Posts	Posts	Tweets	Updates
63,206 character maximum	100,000 character maximum	140 character maximum	700 character maximum
Facebook's "EdgeRank" determines which fans, followers see posts	Post visible to any follower and the public, if desired	Tweets visible to any follower and the public	Posts visible to your connections
Posts can be edited but only within seconds of posting	Posts can be edited	No editing	No editing
Sharing	Re-sharing	Retweeting	
Post likes	+1 voting on posts	Favorites	Update likes
Comment on posts	Comment on posts	Tweets	Comment on updates
Comment likes	+1 on comments	Favorites	Comment likes
Name mentions	+Mentions	@Mentions	
Inline graphics and media	Inline graphics and media	Inline graphics and media	Inline graphics and media
Messages	Post to specific individuals	Direct messages	Direct messages
	Posts in web search results	Tweets in web search results	
1-to-1 video chat (Skype)	Group video chat (Hangout)		
IM chat	Chat	TweetChat	
Unfriend	Block users	Block users	Flag

Fig. 4c

Facebook	Google+	Twitter	LinkedIn
B2C	B2C / B2B	B2C / B2B	B2B

If you're not familiar with the differing features of the major social networks, here is a **social media network comparison chart**: *(fig. 4b)*

Each network has its own pros and cons. Depending on your audience, some networks are more useful than others. Facebook is more relevant for business-to-consumer companies, whereas LinkedIn is better for business-to-business. Google+ and Twitter are so versatile that they are relevant to both B2B and B2C companies. *(fig. 4c)*

Twitter and Analytics

Traffic from Twitter is notoriously difficult to measure. Twitter is a platform-independent network and can be accessed from a huge range of mobile apps and tools, as well as from Twitter.com. But traffic from apps is tracked separately from traffic from websites.

This means that traffic from Twitter may be recorded as coming from a referring site if the click was on Twitter.com or websites like HootSuite.com, but will look like direct traffic if the click was on the Twitter app or HootSuite app.

⚠ **CAUTION!** If you are actively driving traffic to your site through social media, be sure to keep an eye on your mobile stats. Traffic from social media sources is more likely to be from mobile devices (see Mobile in Chapter 3).

In the Lab section in Chapter 4, you'll learn to create content that's more likely to be shared and to promote it quickly using social media channels.

Email Marketing

Although it may now seem like traditional digital marketing, email marketing is a powerful traffic generator. We don't know any serious content marketers who don't use email marketing.

Email creates a pulse in your analytics. Do it regularly and it will look as steady as a heartbeat on an EKG. *(fig. 5)*

Email great for all kinds of businesses. For B2B service companies with long sales cycles, email is a way to keep in touch between purchases and build credibility for leads that are already in the pipeline. For B2C product companies with short decision cycles, a well-timed email can drive sales almost instantly.

Ethical email marketers keep the following principles in mind:

- List growth
- List cleanliness
- Email timing
- Subject lines
- Content and calls to action
- Testing and reporting

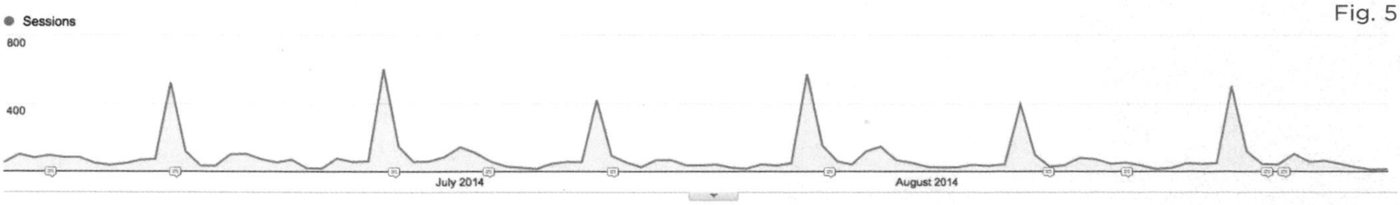

● Sessions
800

400

July 2014   August 2014

Fig. 5

Email Service Providers

Your email service provider (ESP) is the tool you use to create emails and send them to your list. There are hundreds of ESP options to choose from. Some are very inexpensive and cost nothing until you have several thousand subscribers. Others provide a more personalized service, even offering creative design. Here are some general criteria for selecting an ESP:

- **Deliverability**: One of the main functions of an email company is to make sure your emails get through. Unless there's something wrong with your list, you should expect at least 97% of emails to be delivered. These companies have full-time staff dedicated to keeping your email server from getting "blacklisted" by the Hotmails and Gmails of the world. These people have titles like "ISP Relations" and "Director of Deliverability."

- **Easy-to-Use Interface**: The tools you use to manage your list, and create and send an email newsletter, should be simple and require no more time or effort than necessary. None of them are perfect.

- **Reporting**: Without reports, you can't get smarter. And with pretty charts that are easy to read, you're more likely to pay attention and get smarter faster. Reports should be meaningful and compelling. They should show delivery, open and clickthrough rates in ways that make you want to be a better marketer.

TIP! One useful email marketing metric that is rarely emphasized and isn't available within all ESPs is the "click-to-open rate" (sometimes shown as CTOR or CTO). This is the number of unique clicks divided by the number of unique opens. It's useful because it shows how likely people are to engage with your emails after they open them. This removes the variability of open rates and lets you focus on engagement. A CTOR of 20-30% is considered good.

Other criteria for selecting an ESP can include the ability to segment lists, do A/B testing and integrate with a CRM (customer relationship management) system or database of contacts. Of course, price is also relevant!

> "Send timely, targeted, relevant, valuable emails to people who have asked for them." - DJ Waldo *(during an interview on Internet Radio for Smart People)*

With pretty charts that are **easy to read**, you're more likely to pay attention and get smarter faster.

Tracking Traffic from Email Campaigns

The long-term goal of email marketing is to always measure results and continually improve. But unless you add special tracking code, the traffic from your email campaigns will be mixed together with all your other traffic in Google Analytics, making it harder to measure what people are doing after they arrive.

To make the traffic from email appear separately in Google Analytics, use the Google URL Builder. Put each link from your email into this tool, then add the three main parameters into the form: Campaign Source, Campaign Medium and Campaign Name.

Example: You have a website located at www.site.com. You are sending an email newsletter promoting a summer sale. This email will have a link to your home page.

In the URL Builder, enter "newsletter" as the campaign source, "email" as the campaign medium and "summer_sale" as the campaign name. *(fig. 6a)*

Click "Generate URL" and the link changes from http://www.site.com to http://www.site.com/page?**utm_source=newsletter&utm_medium=email&utm_campaign=summer_sale.**

Now, paste the new links generated by this tool into your email. Traffic from this email will appear as a separate source in traffic sources and within the Campaign section. *(fig. 6b)*

Traffic from links that were created using the URL Builder appear as a separate traffic source, shown on this chart as "email."

TIP! The URL Builder can bc used to track links from any source, not just email. Traffic from online ads and social media sources can also be tracked as campaigns. You could even track traffic from QR codes or links in your email signature this way.

In the Lab section, you'll learn the specific aspects of email marketing campaigns that drive results.

Fig. 6a

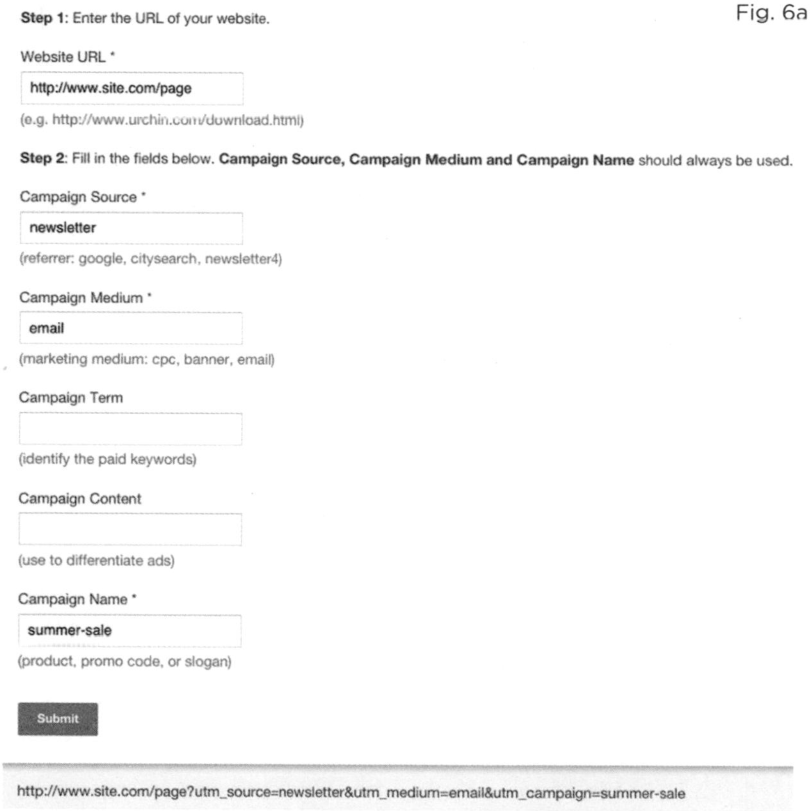

Step 1: Enter the URL of your website.

Website URL *

http://www.site.com/page

(e.g. http://www.urchin.com/download.html)

Step 2: Fill in the fields below. **Campaign Source, Campaign Medium and Campaign Name** should always be used.

Campaign Source *

newsletter

(referrer: google, citysearch, newsletter4)

Campaign Medium *

email

(marketing medium: cpc, banner, email)

Campaign Term

(identify the paid keywords)

Campaign Content

(use to differentiate ads)

Campaign Name *

summer-sale

(product, promo code, or slogan)

Submit

http://www.site.com/page?utm_source=newsletter&utm_medium=email&utm_campaign=summer-sale

☐	1. ■ Organic Search	28,974	66.13%
☐	2. ■ Direct	6,895	15.74%
☐	3. ■ Referral	3,000	6.85%
☐	4. ▨ Social	2,640	6.03%
☐	5. ■ Email	2,201	5.02%
☐	6. ▨ (Other)	104	0.24%
☐	7. ■ Paid Search	1	0.00%

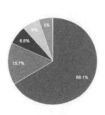

Fig. 6b

Conversions

When a visitor takes action and becomes a lead or customer, the chain reaction is complete. Every form that is filled out and submitted, and every share button that is clicked, is a conversion that can be measured. First, let's look at why visitors convert.

All visitors—all of us—want our problems solved and our desires fulfilled. Maybe we were thinking of the problem or the desire when we came to the site, or maybe not. Either way, *visitors convert into customers when the hope for a solution is stronger than the fear that they'll be disappointed.*

So there are two factors at work: one is pulling them toward conversion and the other is friction that is pushing them away.

Which force is stronger?

If the motivation is stronger than the friction, the visitor converts, meeting their goals and yours.

MOTIVATION
compelling content,
easy to use site,
strong design, trust

FRICTION
weak or unclear content,
unanswered questions,
hard to use site,
lack of trust, confusion

VISITOR

GOAL

Types of Conversions

Generating leads and sales is the ultimate goal of most websites, but there are many types of conversions and all of them are good. The smaller successes are important steps toward turning visitors into fans and fans into customers. *(fig. 7a)*

Subscribers, followers and fans are some of the best conversions because *they allow you to connect with people when they're not on your site*. Now your content can reach farther to people who have asked to receive it, allowing you to drive greater traffic and higher conversions in the future.

Conversion Factors

There are many factors that combine to determine what percentage of visitors convert.

- **Overall design appeal of the site:** Does the site look professional?

- **Relevance**: Are the products or services relevant to the visitor you attracted? How targeted is the website traffic?

- **Clarity of navigation**: Will visitors understand the labeling of links and buttons? Does the navigation layout follow standard web conventions?

Fig. 7a

Conversion Type	Used For	Revenue	Opt-In	Content*
Lead	Lead generation	$		
Customer	eCommerce	$		
Subscribers	Newsletter, RSS		✔	
Event Registrant	Events, webinars			
Donor	Non-profit	$		
Follower / Fan	Social media: - Twitter (follower, Tweet) - Facebook (fan, like) - Google+ (follower, +1) - LinkedIn (follower)		✔	
Member	Account creation: community, directory, forum, ecommerce		✔	
Reviewer	Products, movies, business			*
Commenter	Blog			*
Register to download	eBooks, whitepapers		✔	
Applicant	Recruiting			
Entrant	Sweepstakes, promotions			

*These conversions actually collect content from visitors, which can be repurposed. See Chapter 4 for details.

- **Content quality**: Is the value proposition clear? Is the information useful to the visitor? Does it answer their most important questions? Does it use simple, natural language? Does the content seek first to help, and then to promote the business? (see Content Quality in Chapter 4)

- **Content format**: Is the content presented in visual, compelling format, such as images and video? Is the text-based content legible and formatted for easy scanning and reading?

- **Trust**: Is the website from a known brand? Is there "social proof" or third-party validation, such as lots of Facebook fans, prominent testimonials, positive reviews, BBB rating and industry/association credentials?

- **Compelling calls to action**: Does the site give credible, relevant reasons to take action?

- **Simple, prominent forms**: Are the conversion forms visually prominent? Are the forms short and easy to complete?

TIP! Don't make a testimonials page. When put together on a separate page, testimonials are weaker because they are farther away from the marketing claims that they relate to. Testimonials pages are not likely to be viewed by most visitors.

The more YESes to the above questions, the higher a site's conversion rate will be. Any NOs present obvious problems: distraction, confusion, distrust, annoyance and irrelevance.

Studies show that shorter forms convert at a higher rate. *(fig. 7b)*

TIP! Typically, an overall conversion rate of 3% or more is considered high. If the conversion rate is 1% or lower, something is probably wrong.

Fig. 7b

Short (5 Fields)
Conversion: **13.4%**
Cost per: **$31.24**

First Name: *	
Last Name: *	
Work Email: *	
Company: *	
Job Function: *	Choose One ▾

Medium (7 Fields)
Conversion: **12%**
Cost per: **$34.94**

First Name: *	
Last Name: *	
Work Email: *	
Company: *	
Job Function: *	Select ▾
# Employees: *	Select ▾
Industry: *	Advertising ▾

Long (9 Fields)
Conversion: **10%**
Cost per: **$41.90**

First Name: *	
Last Name: *	
Work Email: *	
Work Phone: *	
Company: *	
Job Function: *	Select ▾
# Employees: *	Select ▾
CRM System: *	Select ▾
Industry: *	Advertising ▾

Source: Marketo: The Definitive Guide to Lead Generation

The better you understand your target audience, the more likely you are to create an online experience that converts well. When possible, create personas, send surveys or do focus group testing. If nothing else, talk to the sales and customer service teams to learn what questions, concerns and objections your potential customers have.

If you can discover the things that pique visitors' interest; create urgency; and address any fears, uncertainties and doubts, you can more easily create a website and develop content that speaks to visitors directly. This is great for your conversion rate.

TIP! Create content that addresses the questions and concerns that are specific to various stages in the buying process and the conversion funnel. More about the sales funnel in Chapter 6.

Short Forms

There is an inverse correlation between the length of a form and the percentage of visitors who fill it out and submit. The more form fields, the lower the conversion rate.

Resist the temptation to create a "warmer lead" by asking for too much information. Long forms are considered "greedy." Often the information you're looking for can be gathered when you follow up on the lead offline. For lead generation forms, include and require the minimum number of fields: name, phone number, email, and possibly company name and message.

NOTE! In some cases, forms need to include questions that allow the website to automatically route the conversion to the right person within an organization. For example, a contact form may route job applicants to HR and leads to the sales team, provided it lets the submitter self-select.

Thank-You Pages and Subsequent Conversions

In our experience designing and building websites at Orbit Media, we have found that the subsequent page after a first conversion is an excellent place to let the visitor take action again. If visitors had enough interest and trust to take action once, they may take action twice if offered the opportunity on the thank-you page.

The trick is to first give visitors what they want. For example, many ecommerce shopping carts ask visitors to create an account before checking out. This isn't what the visitors were hoping for. They clicked "buy now," not "buy after I give you my email address and password."

In the Analytics accounts of our clients, we've seen the lack of a "guest checkout" option *reduces sales by 30-50%*. Requiring visitors to first create accounts is simply greed for more information on the part of a self-centered website owner. This is counter to the principles of content marketing. First, give them what they want. Then, they may give you what you want.

On one website, we added the option to create an account after the checkout process. A simple sentence of benefit copy was right there next to it: "We'll remember your address for a faster checkout next time. We'll also store your order history and let you create a wishlist." The percentage of shoppers who created accounts increased by 40%.

Thank-you pages are often missed opportunities to let the visitor become more engaged.

- A lead generation thank-you page may offer a newsletter sign-up: *"If you'd like to receive our best advice as a monthly email, sign up below."*

- A job applicant thank-you page may offer social media buttons: *"To be the first to know about open positions, follow us on Facebook."*

- An event registration or donation thank you page may offer to let the visitor share the news: *"Share this on Twitter and let your friends know you're going / you donated."*

Even if it doesn't offer a subsequent conversion, the thank-you page can still guide the visitor toward more content with links to pages and posts, rather than being a complete dead end.

Email Sign-Up Forms

"Enter email address" next to a subscribe button isn't exactly a great pitch for your newsletter. On the other hand, if you include the right message next to that sign-up box, you may see a higher conversion rate for subscribers.

- **State the topic**: If the visitor can't tell what the newsletter is going to be about, you aren't conveying the value of subscribing.

- **Indicate frequency**: If the visitor can't tell how often the newsletter is coming, they may hesitate to subscribe.

- **Social proof**: Show the number of subscribers or a testimonial to indicate that others appreciate the content.

Beyond these copy tips, the design of the sign-up box should be visually prominent through color, size and position on the page. We'll take a closer look at email sign-up forms in Chapter 5.

Measure...

As explained in Chapter 1, the percentage of website visitors who take action is called the conversion rate. Conversion rates for each possible conversion on any website should be set up as separate goals within Google Analytics. This will allow you to measure the success of each, and then optimize the site to better convert. This is called Conversion Rate Optimization (CRO).

TIP! Although form submissions are the main type of conversions, Google Analytics can be set up to measure other actions as goal completions. This can include time spent on the website, number of pages viewed, PDF downloads, etc.

Funnel Visualization

To optimize the site for conversions, you need to see where any problems are and what needs to be fine-tuned. To help you see what's happening on and around the conversion pages, Analytics has a report called "funnel visualization."

Fig. 8

		Contact Us Page		
2,974 ▷		**2,974**	▷ **2,645**	
/	1,162		(exit)	1,090
(entrance)	360		/about	227
/about	145	**329 (11.06%)**	/	223
/blog/	143	proceeded to Contact Lead	/portfolio	182
/our-team	137		/contact	174

		Contact Lead
		351
22 ▷		11.72% funnel conversion rate
(entrance)	20	

This report (*fig. 8*) shows how many people came to the Orbit contact form, what pages they came from, how many and what percentage completed the form and, for those that didn't, what pages they visited next.

Note that some of the visitors who didn't convert by completing the form may still have met their own goals and possibly yours. This report doesn't show how many people called you, converting from a visitor to a lead over the phone. The report doesn't show how many people were just looking up your address to send you flowers and a giant check.

⚠️ **WARNING!** If you have an email address on your contact page, but no form, you will not be able to accurately track conversions. There are many disadvantages to simply having an email link, and a serious content marketer would never consider this.

With Google Analytics, it's possible to create longer funnels, or rather, chains of successive funnels. This is useful for ecommerce sites (or any site with forms that take up multiple pages) and allows you track the shopping cart abandonment rate in a more visual report. You'll see how many and what percentage of people progress from the shopping cart to the checkout page to the thank-you page.

...and Improve

Now that you can see this activity, you can begin to look for ways to improve the site to make it more compelling and easier to use. If the number is low, ask yourself the following questions:

- **Did the site answer enough of visitors' initial questions?**
  Talk to the sales team to learn the most common questions and objections. Add content that answers top questions and addresses top concerns.

- **Did the site connect with visitors as people?**
  The site should connect on a human level, through pictures of the team, videos from company leadership, photos of your offices, etc.

- **Does the site convey trust?**
  If not, add third-party credentials, badges for certifications, association memberships, testimonials, case studies, security information (ecommerce) and content that demonstrates experience and expertise.

- **Is the site easy to use?**
  Make sure the forms are short, and pages and sections are named properly. Any tiny bit of confusion between the website and the visitor is friction. The site should guide visitors effortlessly through the series of pages that teaches them, helps them and gently offers to let them take action.

- **Is the content compelling?**
  All the text and video on the top pages must be concise and compelling. When visitors leave the contact form and go to other pages, they're giving you another chance. Make sure those pages are strong (see Content Quality in Chapter 4).

Results are determined by two numbers: traffic and conversions. Traffic times the conversion rate equals leads and revenue. Now that you have a balanced view of both halves of the equation, you can approach web marketing more efficiently. Always try to first diagnose and fix the biggest problems and grab the lowest-hanging fruit.

Lead Generation: Website Best Practices

Now that you have a high-level overview of the success factors, let's go one level deeper into the specifics. Here is a breakdown of how a series of pages and tactics contribute to success in generating leads.

A great lead generation website has a specific set of pages, each with specific elements. Let's break it down. The typical flow looks something like this. *(fig. 9a)*

The website gently leads the visitor through a series of steps: awareness, interest, trust, then action. That's a classic "conversion funnel." Notice how the pages align with steps in the funnel:

A. Blog post: Attracts visitors with useful information (awareness)

B. Web page: Explains what you do (interest)

C. About page: Explains why you do what you do (trust)

D. Contact page: Simple way to get in touch (action)

E. Thank-you page: They've completed the funnel and are now a lead (conversion)

Fig. 9a

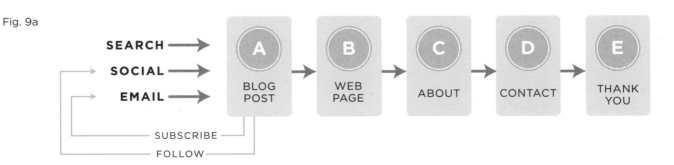

This only works if each page in the process is built for the purpose. Each page needs a set of elements that keeps the process moving.

A. Blog Post: How Can I Help You?

It all starts before the visitor arrives at the website. They may come from email marketing or social media, but often, it starts with a search.

Your audience is constantly looking for information relevant to your field, so the key is to write many helpful blog posts and align the articles with keyphrases. The articles should be so useful that the readers will be glad to have found you.

While they're there, they will find easy ways to get more of your helpful advice through email marketing (a prominent sign-up form), social media (icons that let them follow you) or more content (internal links to related content).

A great blog post is the first step in the lead generation process. It should include all of the following elements. *(fig. 9b)*

1. Keyword-focused header: Use the target keyphrase once in the <h1> header. Along with the <title>, this is one of the most important places to use the phrase.

2. Prominent email sign-up box with descriptive call to action: A great email sign-up form tells people what they're going to get and gives some evidence that it's good.

3. Social media networks, but only those where you are truly active: You don't really want the visitor to leave your site, but if they do, send them to a network where you are truly engaged with your audience.

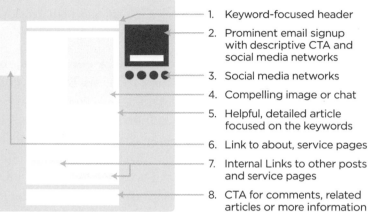

A BLOG POST   Fig. 9b

1. Keyword-focused header
2. Prominent email signup with descriptive CTA and social media networks
3. Social media networks
4. Compelling image or chat
5. Helpful, detailed article focused on the keywords
6. Link to about, service pages
7. Internal Links to other posts and service pages
8. CTA for comments, related articles or more information

4. Compelling image or chart: Every great post has a great image. This makes the post more attractive, both on your site and in the social streams when it gets shared. This is your chance to explain concepts visually with informative charts or diagrams.

5. Helpful, detailed article: It's the deep, how-to content that positions you as the expert. These posts are more likely to rank in search engines and more likely to get shared by readers. So go big. The more useful, the better.

TIP! Don't limit yourself to a certain length. Use as many words as necessary to share the advice and no more. See Chapter 4 for more information about ideal length for website content.

6. Links to service pages and your about page: It's nice of you to give away your best advice, but it's hard work, and it doesn't necessarily generate leads. The pathway from posts to pages should be clear in the navigation.

7. Internal links to other blog posts and service pages: Beyond the navigation, use internal links within your posts to guide visitors deeper into the site, both to other blog posts and to service pages.

8. Call to action for comments, more information: Many visitors may get what they wanted from your super useful blog post and then leave. That's fine, but to improve the chances that they'll stick around, end each post with an invitation to get in touch for more information (link to your contact form) or with a question that invites a comment (see example below).

What's not here: Clutter

Don't show links to old archives, big buttons for various downloads, or special offers. Don't put banner ads for your own business on your website. They're both ugly and distracting..

B. Service Page: Simply What You Do

Here's where you begin selling. Like the blog post, the information here is helpful, but now it describes how you do the work for the prospect. The goal is to state the value you provide in simple terms, and provide evidence that you are legitimate.

These pages must build confidence by giving proof. That may be through examples and data. Testimonials are an excellent way to provide social proof by using the voice of current customers. Service pages need this kind of evidence to support your claims of legitimacy. *(fig. 9c)*

9. Contact link or phone number: The top right corner is the standard place for contact information. Visitors will look for it here. Use either a button to your contact page, your phone number or both.

10. Clear, simple description of services: It's best to call your services what your visitors would call them. Keep the language simple in your headers and body. Make sure to answer the questions that potential customers commonly ask. If you don't, they may look for answers on other websites.

11. Evidence, examples, data and social proof: Anyone can claim to do something, but not everyone can prove it. Add evidence of the benefits and return on investment of your services. This may include examples, statistics and research. Better yet, add social proof in the form of testimonials, using the voice of your happy customers.

12. Videos, demos and diagrams: If you offer a service that requires a high degree of trust, videos are an excellent way to improve lead generation. They let the visitor see your face and hear your voice. If you offer a service that is difficult to explain, use diagrams and demos to explain those complex ideas.

13. Internal links to related services and case studies: As with blog posts, add links within the body to other services or case studies. Unless you have an extremely relevant blog post, you probably shouldn't send visitors from service pages back into the blog.

14. Calls to action: Service pages can either be a dead end, or they can have a quick, friendly call to action, such as "Contact us for more information about (service)."

What's not here:
Secondary conversions

Email sign-up and social media networks have been removed, or at least they aren't as prominent, since you don't want these actions to compete with the more valuable call to action.

C. About Page: Building Trust

Visitors want to know who they might be working with. That's why the "About" page is one of the most popular pages on every lead generation website. Here is where you put a face to the name, tell your story and explain your mission. In the words of Teddy Roosevelt, "Nobody cares how much you know, until they know how much you care."

Connecting the service to the people is critical, even if the organization is large and only the executives are listed here. Visitors who are interested in the service are always interested in the service provider. *(fig. 9d)*

15. Personality, values and your story: Here you'll answer the big questions: Why are you in this business? How long have you been doing this. What motivates your team? Why does this service matter?

You are the only one with your story, so make this a page that sets you apart. You are the only company with your people, so feature them prominently.

16. Testimonials, quotes and awards: Just like the service pages, this is a good place to add evidence of legitimacy. Anything that applies to the entire business

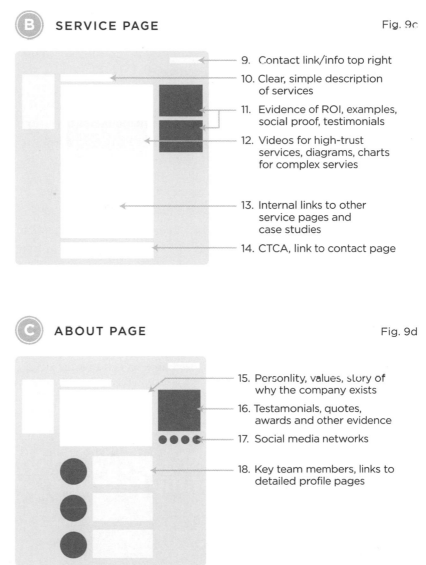

B SERVICE PAGE   Fig. 9c

9. Contact link/info top right
10. Clear, simple description of services
11. Evidence of ROI, examples, social proof, testimonials
12. Videos for high-trust services, diagrams, charts for complex servies
13. Internal links to other service pages and case studies
14. CTCA, link to contact page

C ABOUT PAGE   Fig. 9d

15. Personlity, values, story of why the company exists
16. Testamonials, quotes, awards and other evidence
17. Social media networks
18. Key team members, links to detailed profile pages

"Nobody cares how much you know, until they know **how much you care**."

TEDDY ROOSEVELT

and not just one service will work. That includes awards, certifications, ratings and association memberships, as well as quotes from customers.

17. Social media networks or email sign-up form: This page builds trust, so it's also a good place to let people act. Give them a chance to follow and subscribe.

18. Pictures of key team members with links to detailed profile pages: Don't be a faceless corporation. Be a person. Show the faces of your entire team if you're small and your key leadership if you're big.

What's not here: Everyone's full profile

Link to a separate page for each team member. These pages will show more personality. They may also rank for each person's name.

This is **one of the best tips** for optimizing a website to convert visitors into leads: use a contact form with the minimum number of fields.

D. Contact Page: Where the Magic Happens

The trick here is to get out of the way. It should be as effortless as possible with no distractions. Just a simple form. The idea is to start a conversation, not interrogate your visitors. *(fig. 9e)*

19. Simple contact form: This is one of the best tips for optimizing a website to convert visitors into leads: use a contact form with the minimum number of fields. Of course, you'll need a lot of information to qualify them, but get it during the sales process. Don't use a greedy form.

20. Phone number, address and directions: Not all visitors want to become a web lead. Some want to call. Great. Put all of your contact information on this page, including a link to a map with directions. And If you have an attractive location, show a photo of it here. It helps build legitimacy.

What's not here: Content, navigation, distractions

They're close to the goal, so to keep them moving and remove everything but the form. This page doesn't need any more content! Even the navigation should be kept to a minimum.

E. Thank-You Page: Mission Accomplished

On many lead gen sites, this page is nothing more than two tiny words. That's a missed opportunity. The thank-you page is your first interaction with your new lead.

Make it a good one by setting expectations. You've also got an opportunity here to create an even stronger connection. *(fig. 9f)*

21. A genuine thank-you: Be sincere and use a personal tone. You should also explain what happens next. How soon will you be in touch? Who will make contact?

22. Email sign-up box: If they were ready to reach out, they may already really like you and your brand. Give them the option to subscribe for more of the content that impressed them the first time.

23. Social media networks: Even if they don't follow you, there's still a chance to show them your latest thinking, and a bit of your personality. Just make sure they'll find helpful, relevant posts and positive interactions in your social streams.

24. Links to recommended articles and additional content: If you don't offer other options on this page, you might as well tell people to leave the site. Why not invite them back into your site for a bit more helpful advice?

What's not here: Two lonely little words—thank you.

Yes, lead generation is a bit more complicated than this. Visitors don't necessarily follow that flow. It may take many visits and pageviews over a long timeframe. But do this right and you may feel the difference in your business. Put them all together and you'll make the phone ring and the door swing!

Ⓓ **CONTACT PAGE** Fig. 9e

19. Simple contact form with the minimum number of fields
20. Phone number, address

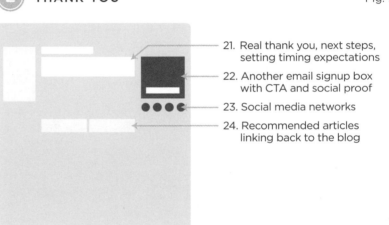

Ⓔ **THANK YOU** Fig. 9f

21. Real thank you, next steps, setting timing expectations
22. Another email signup box with CTA and social proof
23. Social media networks
24. Recommended articles linking back to the blog

Company A's Mobile Visitors

Fig. 10a

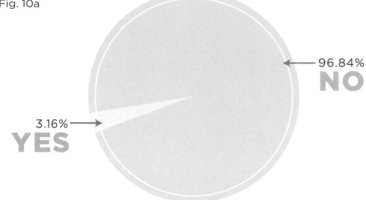

96.84%
NO

3.16%
YES

Company B's Mobile Visitors

Fig. 10b

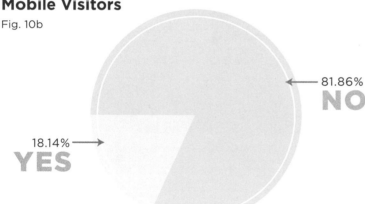

81.86%
NO

18.14%
YES

Special Section: Mobile

Mobile is a mega-trend that can't be ignored. The percentage of visitors who use phones and tablets is increasing daily. This trend isn't slowing down. To get a sense for how this is affecting your website, check your Analytics.

Look at the **Audience > Mobile > Overview** report and view the data as percentages (the pie chart view). Here are some examples of what you might find when you look at what percentage of your visitors are accessing the site from mobile devices: *(fig. 10a and 10b)*

Only 3% of Client A's visitors are using mobile devices, but 18% of Client B's visitors are. Obviously, Client B has a bigger need for a mobile site. But these are extreme examples. Most sites we see are in the 5-7% range for mobile device visitors. These numbers are always higher for companies that are actively involved in email marketing and social media.

Keep in mind that in Google Analytics, mobile visitors include people using tablets as well as phones. But the experience of using a site on an iPad (and most tablet users are still on iPads) is often very similar to the experience on the full site, since even the first edition iPad had a screen resolution of 1024 x 768. This is a size and shape that is similar to the monitor settings on most desktops and laptops.

So look at **Audience > Mobile > Devices** and view the percentages. You'll see that a big chunk of your mobile visitors may be on iPads. *(fig. 10c)*

	Mobile Device Info		Sessions	↓	Sessions	
			12,966		12,966	
			% of Total: 15.15% (85,559)		% of Total: 15.15% (85,559)	
☐	1. Apple iPhone	📷	5,135		39.60%	
☐	2. Apple iPad	📷	2,822		21.76%	
☐	3. (not set)		1,169		9.02%	
☐	4. LG Nexus 5	📷	139		1.07%	
☐	5. HTC M7 One	📷	132		1.02%	

As long as the site doesn't contain Flash (which won't display on iPad and iPhones) or use rollover effects in navigation (there is no mouse cursor on tablets) it may work just fine for these visitors. It's more important that we find out how many visitors are using phones. It's these people who are more likely struggling to navigate and read on a really small screen. (pinch... zoom... scroll... click... oops!... back...)

Let's see what percentage of your visitors are using phones. Take the percentage of total mobile visitors and multiply it by the percentage of non-tablet mobile visitors and you'll see what percentage of your visitors are on phones. In the case of Company B, 18% of visitors are mobile and 60% of those visitors are not on iPads, so around 11% of visitors are using phones.

It's also important to consider the experience our mobile visitors are having. Check to see if these people are sticking around. The "bounce rate" is the percentage of visitors who leave the site after seeing just one page. If the bounce rate for mobile visitors is very high, it's even more important to become mobile-friendly right away.

Mobile	Average Time on Site	% New Visits	Bounce Rate
No	00:05:23	63.73%	41.58%
Yes	00:02:13	60.80%	63.80%

How to Make Mobile Visitors Happy

For years, web designers improved the experience of mobile users by building a separate mobile website. These sites generally lived at a separate address, such as m.website.com or mobile.website.com.

But having a second version of your website often causes problems for managing content. It also risks confusion for search engines. So the latest approach to mobile websites is to build one site that adapts itself depending on the size of the visitor's screen. This is called "responsive web design."

The idea is to design and program the site so that visitors on **all screen sizes**, big and small, have a great experience.

The idea is to design and program the site so that visitors on all screen sizes, big and small, have a great experience. Responsive websites rearrange themselves when the visitor is on a narrow, phone-sized screen, becoming a one-column layout. The navigation is tucked away into an icon in the top right. Phone numbers and addresses become large fingertip-sized buttons that dial the phone and launch map apps.

For tablet users, these websites often show a medium-sized version with touch-friendly navigation. Tablet-friendly websites can't rely on "mouseover" interactions, since tablets don't have mouse cursors.

Best practices for responsive websites are now well established. If you're embarking on a redesign, make sure your site is planned, designed and programmed to be responsive and you'll never worry about your visitors having a good experience, regardless of the device they use.

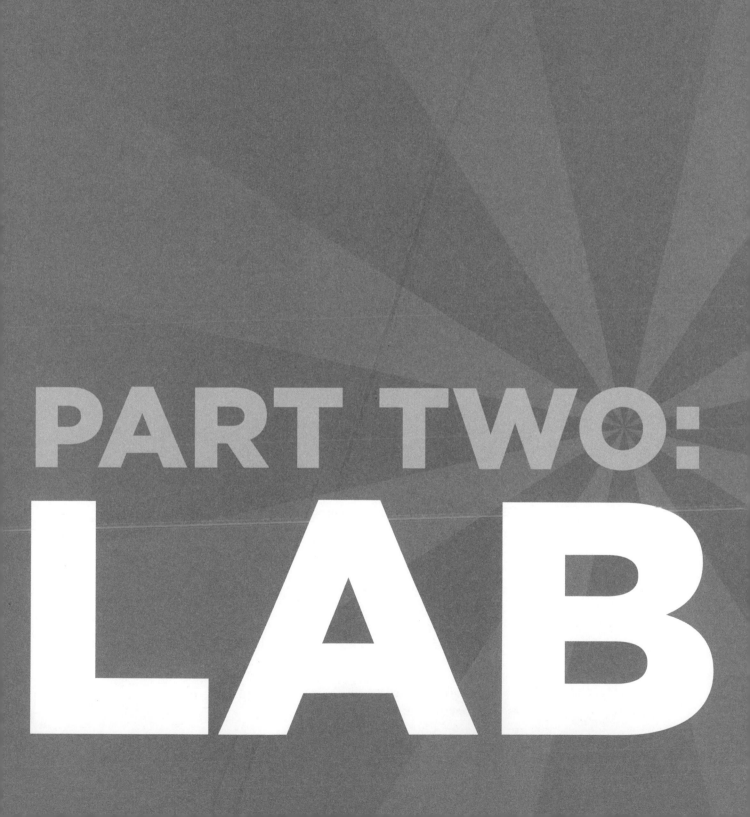

PART TWO:
LAB

Content

The following is a guide to virtually all the types of content on the Internet. It also explains how to quickly create new content by repurposing content you already have.

NOTE! This section is itself an example of repurposed content; it was originally a very popular blog post on the Orbit site. It's been viewed and shared thousands of times and was translated into French and German.

Atomize Your Content: The Periodic Table of Content

Content is made up of pieces. And pieces can be broken down into smaller pieces or combined into larger pieces, just like the elements on the Periodic Table. Thinking about content as particles will give you ideas on how to quickly create new content by "atomizing" your existing content into smaller pieces or combining content into larger compounds.

But before you turn your articles into particles, let's look at what the content universe is made of. Once we know what's on the Periodic Table of Content *(fig. 11)*, we'll be ready to start smashing particles in the content accelerator.

What follows is a description of each particle and examples of how to break it down or combine it with others. If you don't want to read them all, just look at the ones you already have and the ones you want to create.

 Tw (Tweet): A tiny particle that survives in nature only a short time. Tweets are known for traveling far and in many directions, and they may be comprised of subatomic links, mentions, hashtags and quotes.

- *Any content can be atomized into Tweets*. Doing so can lead to small chain reactions of shares and clicks. Quotes, stats, captions and headlines can all be made into Tweets.

Fig. 11

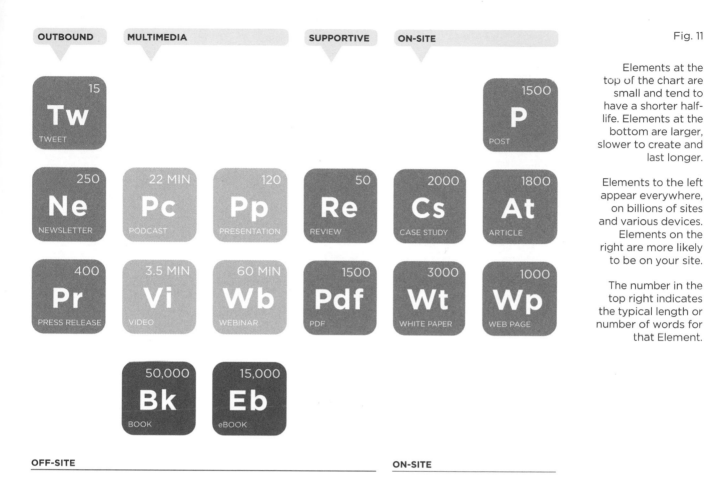

OUTBOUND	MULTIMEDIA		SUPPORTIVE	ON-SITE	
Tw 15 TWEET					**P** 1500 POST
Ne 250 NEWSLETTER	**Pc** 22 MIN PODCAST	**Pp** 120 PRESENTATION	**Re** 50 REVIEW	**Cs** 2000 CASE STUDY	**At** 1800 ARTICLE
Pr 400 PRESS RELEASE	**Vi** 3.5 MIN VIDEO	**Wb** 60 MIN WEBINAR	**Pdf** 1500 PDF	**Wt** 3000 WHITE PAPER	**Wp** 1000 WEB PAGE
	Bk 50,000 BOOK	**Eb** 15,000 eBOOK			

OFF-SITE _____ ON-SITE _____

Elements at the top of the chart are small and tend to have a shorter half-life. Elements at the bottom are larger, slower to create and last longer.

Elements to the left appear everywhere, on billions of sites and various devices. Elements on the right are more likely to be on your site.

The number in the top right indicates the typical length or number of words for that Element.

- Tweets can be combined into a post. For example, use three Tweets and add your own commentary, or simply list 12 related Tweets.

P (Post): As primary building blocks of web content, Posts can be seen as updates on social media sites (Facebook, G+) or in corporate blogs or other streams. They tend to be timely,

- Since Posts are already small, they can only be broken down into Tweets.

- Posts are strongest in compounds with other elements. Link to posts from Tweets and Newsletters. Link from Posts to Web Pages.

Ne (Newsletter): An outbound particle that lives slightly longer than the Tweet. It has more properties, including subject lines and link tracking, so it requires careful handling.

- Newsletters should always link to Posts and Articles. Their energy is lower unless this bond is created. If a Newsletter gives the full text and doesn't link to something else, the visitor doesn't click and no traffic is generated. Never put the full text into a newsletter. Always combine!

Pc (Podcast): The Podcast is pure, distilled audio and has no visual energy. Podcasts are typically less powerful than Video, but more powerful than text because of their ability to convey tone. Create them using radio frequency microphone technology.

- Podcasts are easy to create by recording readings of Articles and Case Studies.

- Podcasts may be byproducts of the Presentation creation process. Simply pull the audio track out of a Video or Webinar, or record the presentation using a smartphone and edit later.

Pp (Presentation): No longer viewed only on projectors during speeches, today Presentations can now be found across the web, ranking in searches and shared through social media. They are most powerful when charged with visual content like charts and images.

- Post Presentations to Slideshare and embed them in Web Pages, including LinkedIn.

- Record the audio track to create a Podcast.

- If possible, use social media coverage to live-Tweet those juicy sound bites during the presentation. Use a predetermined hashtag sub-particle.

Re (Reviews): Also known as recommendations or testimonials. Since the recent explosion of these particles, Reviews can be found everywhere. Find them on your Yelp page, LinkedIn, Google+ Local page or free-roaming emails.

- Combine them with your Web Pages through testimonial chemistry, but never create a Web Page of testimonials. Reviews are supportive content that increase the credibility of other particles. When they stand alone (on a testimonials page) they are weaker, since reading reviews is typically not the main reason why people visit websites. They go to get information and learn.

- Add Reviews to Case Studies, Newsletters and Press Releases.

Cs (Case Study): Sometimes known as "success stories," Case Studies increase credibility and are useful when trust is critical and the sales process is long. The problem-solution-result structure is easy to spot. Case Studies are powerful because they can be atomized into almost anything.

- Break them down into outbound Newsletters, less formal Articles and two or three Tweets to increase traffic.

- Combine with Reviews (use the Testimonial isotope) and link to Web Pages to increase conversions.

Case Studies are powerful because they can be atomized into **almost anything**.

At (Article): An extremely versatile element, Articles are slightly larger and more structured than Posts. They are less self-serving than Web Pages. Articles are created to inform and entertain, not just market and promote.

- Atomize Articles into Posts and Tweets.

- Transform into Web Pages (add product/service information) or Case Studies (restructure, add example).

- Combine 5 articles into an eBook or 20 articles into a Book.

Pr (Press Release): This targeted, highly-charged particle travels quickly. Although it was once directed specifically at media, today it can be found ranking in search engines and reaching a wider spectrum.

- Press Releases are easy to convert into Web Pages and Articles, but be careful. Rewrite the Press Release before posting it on your site to avoid the duplicate content penalty. Each Web Page particle on your site should be original and unique on the web.

Vi (Video): Although the content and messaging may overlap with surrounding particles, the format stands alone as one of the most compelling and powerful formats for content.

- Most content can be atomized into Video in any properly equipped lab.

- Video becomes more powerful when bonded to a Web Page (a process known as "embedding"), which improves the page's conversion rate (visitors into leads).

Wb (Webinar): Similar to a Presentation, but always with audio and sometimes with video. When viewed in real time and given a hashtag, Webinars often generate Tweets.

- Create Video or Podcast particles through recording technology.

- If the Webinar requires registration, be sure to atomize a summary or transcription. Make it viewable as an Article for people who weren't able to attend the live version.

TIP! When Webinars require registration/subscription, subsequent Newsletter particles have greater energy and reach.

Pdf (PDF files): These are supportive particles that should never stand alone. Any valuable content that is currently within a PDF but not on a Web Page should be atomized immediately, since PDFs are not search friendly and lack Analytics.

- Best when bonded to Web Pages as alternate (print-friendly, downloadable) versions of Articles, White Papers, Press Releases, etc.

- There are only a few specific environments where PDFs can stand alone and still have value: Scribt and Slideshare.

Wt (White Paper): Also referred to as a Research Report, Technical Brief, or Guide, White Papers tend to be formal, text heavy and a bit boring. Historically common, many White Papers still exist in legacy content and sometimes they are relevant for years. *These are prime candidates for atomization.*

- One White Paper can often be broken down into three or more Article or Posts.

- If the White Paper is available only as a PDF, make it into a set of Web Pages.

- Post on Scribd.

- If there is an Executive Summary, this may be broken off into a Case Study or Web Page.

- Subatomic quotes and stats can become Tweets.

Wp (Web Page): A stable particle that's clear, direct and easy to control. Its effectiveness is also easy to measure. Web Pages are powerful in both search engine marketing and converting visitors into leads and customers. They are not frequently shared on their own, however.

Case Studies, Articles and White Papers should all be atomized into Web Pages.

Marketing PDFs should always be converted into web pages.

Reviews should not be combined into a Web Page since "testimonial" pages generate disproportionately low visits. Reviews should be added to various pre-existing web pages.

Bk (Book): Offline particle with a history of endurance. No particle is older except the ancient Scroll (Sc) and Slab (Sl).

- Books can be created by combining many Article particles through editing fusion. This process releases large amounts of credibility.

- Books can be atomized into Articles and White Papers.

Eb (eBook): Similar to the Book but shorter. Similar to the White Paper, but less formal and text-heavy. eBooks typically feature more design elements (charts and images) and can be created easily using presentation software such as Powerpoint or Keynote.

- Convert White Papers into eBooks.

- Combine Articles with a similar theme into an eBook.

TIP! When eBook downloads require registration/subscription, subsequent Newsletter particles have greater energy and reach.

Atom-Smashing Examples (Good and Bad)

Multiplying Video (good): Brad Farris of EnMast made a one hour Webinar interview of three experts. Later, he atomized the video into three shorter Videos, each focused on one expert answering a specific question.

Atomic Meltdown (bad): A biomedical company hired a PR firm that used the company's home Web Page as a press release and submitted it to online news wires. The explosion in duplicate content caused Google to blacklist the domain. *The company no longer ranked, even for its own name.* Hazmat suits and a reconsideration request were needed to clean up.

Final Thesis

Content marketing is exactly like high-energy physics. Well, not really. But you can accelerate your publishing if you look at the content around you and think about combining things and breaking things down....a webinar becomes a podcast...the podcast becomes a blog post...combine the blog post with a newsletter...etc.

Create an inventory to see what you have. Group your content into topics and elements. See if anything is missing or if anything can be atomized quickly.

Be a web marketing scientist, find something to atomize, and make your marketing go boom.

Content Development: How to Write

Yes, video and audio content are wonderful, but we're going to focus on text content here. Writing is absolutely essential in web marketing. You must write to be a content marketer.

Channels

Start by considering where and how the content will be published. You have four main options:

1. Web page
2. Blog post
3. Blog post and newsletter
4. Guest post

Here is a summary of the differences between these channels and how they relate to publishing:

1. **Web page**: If you don't have a blog, this may be your only option for publishing content. If you do have a blog, this may still be a good choice. If the piece you're writing is focused on a key product or service, or if it contains critical information for anyone making a purchasing decision, it probably should be an actual web page on your site rather than a post within the blog.

    Although web pages should be informative and useful to readers, they are typically more marketing-focused. Here's where you're selling as much as teaching.

2. **Blog post**: These are similar to web pages, but are date-stamped and associated with an author. The tone may be more informal. If your website is a newspaper, the blog is where op-ed pieces will go. They should be useful and informative, not salesy or marketing-focused. Here's where you're teaching, more than selling.

    Unlike web pages, blog posts should have a conversational tone that invites comments. Great blog posts are the starting point for a conversation that continues in the comments beneath.

NOTE! Although web pages and blog posts are listed separately, the blog should be embedded in a website within the same domain. The ideal place for a blog is www.website.com/blog. Hosting a blog using a subdomain is also good, such as blog.website.com. I do not recommend blogging on a separate domain such as myblog.blogspot.com since your website will not get a link popularity (search marketing) benefit from any inbound links to your blog posts.

3. **Blog post and newsletter**: Some blog posts are promoted using email marketing. These should contain your best content and be on a topic that your subscribers find interesting.

WARNING! *Don't send full-text newsletters.* Note that there is no option for newsletter-only. Email marketing is a great way to get your content out there, but if you put the full text of your content in the email itself, your subscribers can get the full value of the piece without clicking. No click = no traffic to your website.

Newsletters should include an excerpt from the article or a short summary, and then link to the full text on your website with a compelling call to action. This will allow you to measure clickthrough rates, solicit comments, encourage sharing and convert subscribers into leads and customers.

4. **Guest post / external website:**: Same as any blog post, but published on a website other than your own. Guests posts may not be as tightly focused on your usual topics. If you write something that you find interesting but your typical visitors may not, consider finding a home for it on another site. Guest blogging is a powerful link building tactic that will be discussed in more detail in Chapter 5.

WARNING! *Duplicate content:* Note that there is also no option for a combination blog post and guest post. If you post the same article on your site and on other sites, Google might not be able to tell which is the original. It may get confused and rank the wrong version, or rank neither.

Even worse, Google may perceive the multiple versions of your content as an attempt at spam. In extreme cases, this can lead to your domain being blacklisted (i.e., removed from Google's index permanently). This is a death sentence for search traffic.

At Orbit, one of our clients launched a site and simultaneously hired a PR firm to promote it. Rather than write an original press release, the PR firm simply copied the text from the website homepage and submitted it to the online newswires. Within minutes, there were more than 1,000 instances of that home page content on the web.

Google flagged this as likely spam and blacklisted the domain. Suddenly, the website disappeared from search results, even for searches for the business name.

Imagine not ranking for the name of your business. Devastating.

The client blamed Orbit and, although we hadn't caused the problem, we were able to repair it by filing a reconsideration request that explained what happened. The Google web spam team manually removed the domain from the blacklist.

To avoid a possible duplicate content penalty, be sure that all of the content on your website is original.

How original is original? The threshold for "original" is likely around 25%. In other words, no web pages or posts on your site should be more than 25% the same as other pages and posts on the web or you may risk a penalty. If you are ever tempted to summarize another post on your site (or write a summary of one of your posts when guest blogging) don't use an excerpt of more than one fourth of the original article.

Keyphrase Research

Believe it or not, I research keyphrases before writing almost anything. Since it's not difficult or time consuming, it's foolish not to align your content with a keyphrase for which people are searching. Rather than simply writing content on a topic you find interesting, you can write content on a topic you find interesting and people are looking for.

Investigating keyphrases is like reading the minds of millions of people. It may sound strange, but I look up the popularity of words and phrases almost every day. It's truly amazing the things you can learn within minutes:

To avoid a possible **duplicate content penalty**, be sure that all of the content on your website is original.

- You'll find out what people really call your products or services, helping you to avoid using jargon and ensure you're using phrases that are top-of-mind for your audience when you talk about your business.

- You'll discover which related services and products people are looking for, helping you to consider expanding your offerings (or at least your content).

- You'll know where people are looking for your services and products, helping you to understand where the demand is and whether you should expand or adapt.

With two minutes of research, I can tell which cities in the U.S. have the most people looking for Botox treatments. I can tell you what questions people have about tree trimming. I can tell which times of year people are looking for math tutors. I can tell you whether interest in vegetarian dog treats is increasing or decreasing. I've seen clients decide to add new products and open stores in new locations based on this research.

As a content marketer, the two primary uses for keyphrase research are to find phrases to include in your content and to get ideas for new content. By doing keyphrase research, you'll create content that is more friendly for search engines and more relevant to your audience.

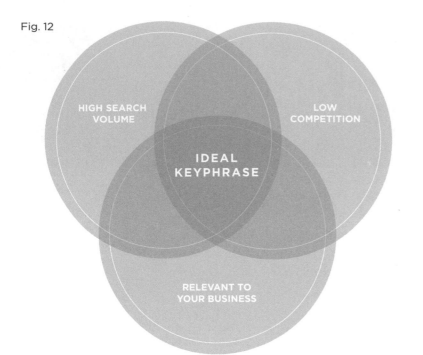
Fig. 12

HIGH SEARCH
VOLUME

LOW
COMPETITION

IDEAL
KEYPHRASE

RELEVANT TO
YOUR BUSINESS

Check Search Volume (Popularity)

Although there are many tools that show how popular various keyphrases are, I recommend the Google tools because they have the most data. The two tools we'll use here are Google AdWords Keyword Planner and Google Trends. They're very different, but they complement each other. Let's compare.

- **Google AdWords Keyword Planner**: Suggests many phrases and shows estimated numbers for monthly search volume (how many people are searching for the phrase) in the U.S. and around the world.

- **Google Trends**: Shows trending for specific phrases over time. Allows comparison of phrases and also suggests a few phrases.

The ideal keyphrases are those that meet three criteria: many people are searching for them (high search volume), the website has a realistic chance of ranking relative to other sites (low competition) and the page that would rank is relevant to your business. *(fig 12)*

Assuming we know what topics and keywords are relevant, let's focus on the first two criteria:

- **Search volume:** This is the popularity of the keyword. How many people are searching for the phrase? There is no point in targeting a phrase if no one is searching for it.

- **Competition:** There is also no point in targeting a phrase if you have no chance of ranking for it. How likely is your page to rank for the phrase? How many websites are relevant for this phrase? Are they powerful sites?

	Google Keyword Planner	Google Trends
Suggested phrases	Up to 800	10
Search volume displayed as	Specific numbers (estimates)	Trending (line graph)
Geography	Countries, states, regions, cities	Countries, states, metro areas

The Keyword Planner is your bread and butter for research, but Google Trends is a great complement.

Google AdWords Keyword Planner

Here's where we narrow down a universe of possible phrases to the one or two on which you'll eventually focus on. The goal is to disqualify the phrases with too few searches (the invisible) or too much competition (the impossible).

NOTE! This tool is known to leave out some data in the suggested keyphrases, so if you have a good feeling about a phrase, enter it manually if you don't see it suggested.

1. Start Wide: Enter several possible phrases into the box at the top of the page and click Search. Here's an example of the results for the phrase "HVAC repair." *(fig. 13)*

At the top of the list, you'll see the specific phrase you entered, along with the average number of monthly searches over the last year. This is the "search volume."

WARNING: The "competition" column on this list is not competition within the organic Google search results, but rather competition within Google AdWords. That's because this tool is actually intended to be a tool for AdWords advertisers. In many cases, keyphrases listed as "Low" may have little competition in AdWords Pay-Per-Click advertising, but are actually highly competitive and would be difficult to rank for in organic SEO.

As you review the wide range of related phrases, you're looking for two things: phrases that more specifically relate to your topic and

Fig. 13

| Ad group ideas | Keyword ideas | | | | | | ~ | ↓ Download | Add all (801) |

Search terms		Avg. monthly searches ?	Competition ?	Suggested bid ?	Ad impr. share ?	Add to plan
hvac repair	~	2,900	High	$25.84	0%	»

1 - 1 of 1 keywords ▾   〈   〉

Keyword (by relevance)		Avg. monthly searches ?	Competition ?	Suggested bid ?	Ad impr. share ?	Add to plan
hvac service and repair	~	10	High	$13.97	0%	»
air conditioning repairman	~	50	High	$17.29	0%	»
heating air conditioning company	~	20	High	$29.55	0%	»
heating & air conditioning repair	~	90	High	$30.15	0%	»
heating and air conditioning contractor	~	10	High	$17.59	0%	»
heater and air conditioner repair	~	30	High	-	0%	»

completely new phrases that have a similar meaning, especially those with high search volume. Add these to your original list.

2. Find Keywords from Other Sources: If you need ideas for topics and keywords, consider these tools and sources:

- **Google Analytics**: Find phrases and topics that are already driving traffic by looking in Traffic Sources > Search Engine Optimization > Queries. Keywords related to these will be easier for ranking.

- **Google Suggest**: Just begin entering relevant keywords into Google and see what phrases Google suggests. Try first entering question words like "how to" and "what," along with your topic, for more suggestions. You might get new ideas for phrases with good search volume.

- **Ubersuggest:** Here's a way to see all kinds of Google suggestions. Ubersuggest.org scrapes Google for every possible suggestion that starts with the word or phrase you provided. Brilliant.

⬆ air conditioning

⊕ air conditioning
⊕ air conditioning repair
⊕ air conditioning units
⊕ air conditioning service
⊕ air conditioning contractors of america
⊕ air conditioning bypass
⊕ air conditioning filters
⊕ air conditioning history
⊕ air conditioning parts
⊕ air conditioning vent covers

- **Talk to your team**: People within your organization are a great source for keyword ideas. Talk to people involved in sales and customer service to find out what topics they've been talking about. Align a topic with a phrase, and ask if they wouldn't mind writing the article!

Enter your new keyword ideas into the Keyword Planner to check the search volume.

How many searches are enough?
For most businesses, it's ideal if the main keyphrase for your site has thousands of searches per month. The home page should be optimized for this phrase. Interior pages, such as product and service pages, should be optimized for more specific phrases. Those phrases may have hundreds of searches per month. Search volume for a blog post's target keyphrase may be even lower, with fewer than 100 searches per month.

What about long keyphrases?
For businesses where the value of a potential transaction is high, such as a B2B service company, it may be useful to target very specific phrases with very few searches. If only 30 people search for a phrase each month, that's still a potential visitor every day. Long, very specific search phrases, such as entire questions, are referred to as "long tail" keyphrases.

These phrases may have little, if any, competition. If you target a long tail phrase with six or seven words, it's possible that you'll have the only page on the Internet with that combination of those words together in that order. You may rank high within days of posting the content and the visitors may be highly targeted. A few hours of content marketing today may lead to a steady trickle of traffic and a handful of qualified leads for years to come.

Can I target more than one phase?
What about secondary keyphrases?
It's unlikely that a single page will rank high for many phrases, especially a blog post. For this reason, it's best to target one keyphrase. You may have success targeting more than one phrase, if the phrases have words in common. This is easier if the phrases share the first word or two, rather than the last. If the primary and secondary keyphrases are completely dissimilar, the page is less likely to rank for both.

3. Search for the Phrase: The only way to really gauge the competition for a given phrase is to search for it. As you do this, keep in mind that search results are personalized for you and may not be similar to what someone else sees. Here are three tips get a better sense for what "typical" search results might be for a given phrase when you're checking competition in Google:

1. Make sure you're logged out of Google+.

2. Set the location to the location for your target audience. Leave it set for your city if your audience is local. Set it to "United States" for a national audience.

3. If you're really skeptical of the search results you're seeing, visit www.google.com/adpreview to search Google with fewer of the signals that are specific to you and your computer.

Search results may vary
Now you should be looking at a search engine results page (or "SERP" as the SEOs like to say). The last few years have brought much more diversity in the types of content in search results, so there's a good chance you're seeing images, news, video, local listings and, of course, ads. All of these are in addition to the usual organic listings. They are called "blended" or "universal" search results.

⚠️ **CAUTION!** Searching for some phrases will return local search results. If there's a map in the top right corner and the search results page is dominated by a group of local listings (usually in a group of seven or three), the usual search engine optimization efforts aren't going to be enough. You'll need to do Local SEO, which is not based on content marketing.

Your local listing in Google is a Google+ Local page. To improve the ranking of this page in the local listings, make sure that your business information is up to date on all of the Internet Yellow Pages websites (IYPs) and anywhere else where you have a business listing. Sites that show your business name and address are called "citations." Submit your business to IYPs and directories to create more citations and improve the rank of your Google+ Local page. Consider everything from Yelp and Merchant Circle to local directory sites and chambers of commerce. Positive reviews may also affect the rank of a Google+ Local page.

📓 **NOTE!** Google often shows search results for general meanings, rather than specific words and phrases. When you search for a phrase in Google, you'll see the keyword bolded in the search results. Look closely and you may find words you didn't search for, bolded in those same search results. For example, a search for "HVAC repair" returns search listings with phrases such as "heating" and "air conditioning."

Google engineers call this "semantic indexing." Google shows pages that include words that are semantically linked to the words in your search. Often, they're actual synonyms. Keep this in mind as you measure competition.

> Google often shows search results for general meanings, rather than **specific words and phrases**.

4. Estimate the Competition: In my opinion, this is one of the more difficult web marketing skills. It's tricky. There are many tools that try to make it easier. Some tools show a score called "Keyword Effectiveness Index," which combines search volume and competition. Moz estimates competition with a "Keyword Difficulty" score. But I find it best to check competition manually, without tools.

Take a look at the search engine results page for the phrase you're researching. Here are some keyword research tips for determining competition. The phrase is likely competitive if:

- There are ten pay-per-click ads on the page, three at the top and seven down the side. This means others have already determined the keyphrase is valuable.

- There are tens of millions of results. This means there are many pages on the web that are relevant for this phrase.

- The top-ranking sites have the target keyphrase at the beginning of the link. This means those sites have the keyphrases at the beginning of their page titles, which indicates the owners of these sites know a bit of SEO.

- The top-ranking sites are popular, well-known sites. Unless you invent a time machine, you're not going to outrank Wikipedia. If the top three or five sites are trusted, reputable websites, they'll have loads of link popularity and therefore powerful domains. You're not likely to compete without focusing serious time and resources. More information on how to estimate the authority of a domain in Chapter 5: Guest Blogging.

Still unsure if you have a chance of ranking? Try this: check the "domain authority" of the top-ranking and bottom-ranking sites on page one in Google. Enter both sites into OpenSiteExplorer.org. If the domain authority of your site is in that range, you should have a chance of ranking. Keep in mind, unless you're an Moz subscriber, you can only use this tool three times per day.

TIP! The MozBar is a browser plugin that shows you the authority of all the pages on a search results page. Search for any phrase, then select "Show SERP Overlay" in the toolbar. This will show you the authority of the pages and domains for each listing, right there within the search results.

Shortcut!

Here's how to research keywords fast. You can estimate your odds of ranking based on your Domain Authority and the keyword search volume. This is a shorthand way to quickly research keywords for which you can reasonably expect to rank.

Fig. 14

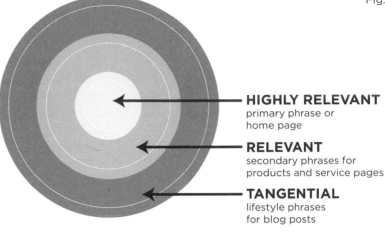

HIGHLY RELEVANT
primary phrase or
home page

RELEVANT
secondary phrases for
products and service pages

TANGENTIAL
lifestyle phrases
for blog posts

If your Domain Authority is...	Target keyphrases with monthly searches of...
less than 30	less than 100
less than 50	less than 1000
less than 70	less than 3000

TIP! If you really want to rank, but the phrase is too competitive and your site's domain isn't powerful enough, consider submitting it as a guest post to a blog with a more authoritative domain.

Relevance

It should go without saying that there is a third criteria for choosing keyphrases: Relevance. It's pointless to target a phrase that is completely irrelevant to your business.

The ideal phrase is highly relevant to a problem your business solves for people. This phrase brings them to content that teaches something about the problem or solution. The more relevant the phrase and valuable the content, the higher the conversion rate from these visitors will be. *(fig. 14)*

But phrases and content that are only indirectly related to your business can also drive traffic—and eventually leads. It just has to be useful to the visitor and somehow related to what you offer.

- Bad indirect targeting: Real estate company targets the name of a nearby college.

- Good indirect targeting: Real estate company targets phrase with the community name and education-related phrases.

Even "low-quality" visitors can be valuable. They may share your content, subscribe to your newsletter, follow you on Twitter, comment on a post or link to you from their blog. Every visit is a chance for something good to happen.

Case Study: Graphic Design vs. Web Design
In June 2010, Nick Haas, Orbit's Creative Director, had an idea for an article. He wanted to describe the difference between traditional graphic design and the kind of web design done at Orbit.

Rather than simply write a great blog post, we took a few minutes to do the research using the Keyword Tool. We discovered that the phrase "graphic design vs. web design" is searched 58 times per month.

When checking competition in Google, there didn't seem to be any popular domains ranking high. The sites that were ranking didn't seem to be well optimized (i.e., they didn't have the phrase at the beginning of their title). It seemed we had found a very specific phrase with relatively low search volume but with very low competition. Bingo.

So Nick wrote the article with the phrase in mind. The article is just as informative and well written as it would have been without this research, but now it was destined to rank. For details on exactly how to include the phrase on the page in the appropriate places, see the Article Checklist section later in this chapter.

Nick's article, *Graphic Design vs. Web Design: Separate and Not Equal,* went live on June 22, 2010. In less than a week, it was ranking like a champion. It's been in the first or second position for that phrase ever since. For the first few months, it was visited once or twice a day. Then a few sites began linking to it and traffic increased. When a high-profile blog linked to it, it jumped again.

NOTE! The boost in link popularity to this individual blog post benefits the trust and authority of the entire orbitmedia.com domain, and potentially helps the rank of all the pages on the site.

Since the post went live, it's been visited more than 14,500 times. Recently, it has received 6-7 visits per day, and 25% of that traffic comes from social sharing and referring sites. *(fig. 15a)*

A bit of keyphrase research goes a long way.

Google Trends

When you have a sense of what phrases you plan to target, take a minute to validate those phrases using Google Trends. Here is an example of the two main ways to use it.

Suppose you're a web design company (just imagine!) and you're creating a page about a new service for marketing your clients' websites. But should you call it web marketing, digital marketing or internet marketing?

1. Visit Google Trends.

2. Enter those three phrases.

3. Choose "United States" as a filter.

4. Click "search."

Here's what you'll see... *(fig. 15b)*

Keyphrase Trending: Ohh! Charts!

Although "internet marketing" is the more popular phrase, you can see that sometime during the summer of 2011, "digital marketing" became a more popular phrase than "web marketing." Had you researched these phrases in early 2011 using only the Google Keyword Planner, you may have concluded that "web marketing" is a better phrase than "digital marketing." Not so today!

Fig. 15a

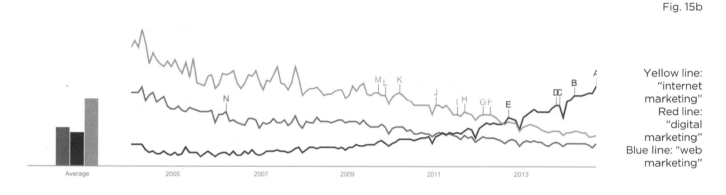

- Pageviews

500

250

July 2011   January 2012   July 2012   January 2013   Ju

Primary Dimension: Page Other ▾

Plot Rows | Secondary dimension ▾ | Sort Type: Default ▾ | 🔍 advanced

Page		Pageviews	Unique Pageviews	Avg. Time on Page	Entrances	Bounce Rate	% Exit
		7,271	6,521	00:04:17	6,439	88.45%	86.19%
		% of Total: 1.01% (721,732)	% of Total: 1.08% (602,067)	Site Avg: 00:01:50 (134.32%)	% of Total: 1.80% (357,734)	Site Avg: 66.18% (33.63%)	Site Avg: 49.57% (73.89%)
1.	/blog/graphic-design-vs-web-design-separate-and-not-equal	7,271(100.00%)	6,521(100.00%)	00:04:17	6,439(100.00%)	88.45%	86.19%

Fig. 15b

Yellow line: "internet marketing"
Red line: "digital marketing"
Blue line: "web marketing"

Average   2005   2007   2009   2011   2013

Seeing this trend, especially with the forecast, it's clear which of the two is the more popular phrase. I have often been surprised by keyphrase trending.

TIP! *Seasonality affects trends.* Since the data goes back to 2004, you can see seasonal trends for various phrases. You'll notice that most phrases have seasonality. With some phrases, it's dramatic.

When you have a sense of what phrases you plan to target, take a minute to **validate those phrases** using Google Trends.

Regional interest ⑦

Worldwide > United States

web marketing digital marketing internet marketing

Subregion | Metro | City

Vermont	100
Utah	100
Nevada	89
Colorado	89
Florida	86
California	85
Arizona	83

▸ View change over time ⑦   </>   </>

- "Web marketing" search popularity across the U.S.: Search volume is distributed relatively evenly.

Regional interest ⑦

Worldwide > United States

web marketing **digital marketing** internet marketing

Subregion | Metro | City

New York	100
New Jersey	80
Illinois	77
Connecticut	74
Massachusetts	73
California	67
Michigan	60

▸ View change over time ⑦   </>   </>

- "Digital marketing" search popularity across the U.S.: Mostly in states with major metropolises.

Regional interest ⑦

Worldwide > United States

web marketing digital marketing **internet marketing**

Subregion | Metro | City

Nevada	100
Florida	85
Utah	82
Arizona	78
Colorado	70
California	68
Georgia	61

▸ View change over time ⑦   </>   </>

- "Internet marketing" search popularity across the U.S.: Usage of this keyphrase is much stronger in Florida and Nevada than in other states.

Conclusion? Start an internet marketing company in Nevada.

I'm kidding. Going back to the page you're planning to write, consider using the target keyphrase "internet marketing." But if the phrase is too competitive, or if you are looking for a secondary phrase, target "digital marketing." Adjust based on your state or metro area.

You may not have time to check all your target phrases this way, but always check your main phrases. Should you check a keyphrase for a blog post? Maybe not. But a phrase for your home page, service pages or product pages? Absolutely!

- Target phrases that are trending up whenever possible.
- Target phrases that are popular in your region whenever possible.

Now that you're an expert at keyphrase research, it's time to learn how to incorporate target phrases into your content.

Can I target more than one phrase? What about secondary keyphrases?
Pages tend to rank higher in search engines when they are tightly focused on a single topic. It's unlikely that one page will rank high for a dozen phrases. So if we expect to rank, we need to pick a phrase and create a great page on that topic.

But what about just two phrases? Can we optimize a page for a primary and secondary keyword? Yes. But only if we pick phrases that meet one of these two criteria:

1. Two phrases with overlapping words: Ideally, the two keyphrases share words. Even better, the primary keyword is a subset of the secondary keyword. Here are some examples:

- **Bad**: *"Social media for beginners"* and *"Twitter tips"*: These phrases may share a meaning, but they don't share any words.

- **Good**: *"How to research keywords"* and *"Keyword research tips"*: These two phrases both share two words, keyword and research, but the words appear in different order within the phrases.

- **Better**: *"Google Authorship markup"* and *"Google Authorship"*: Here, the second phrase is contained within the first phrase. One phrase is really just a more specific version of the other.

2. Two phrases with similar semantics and synonyms: When you searched for your initial phrase in step three above, did you see any different, but related words or phrases bolded in the search results? If so, you've found an example of Google using semantic indexing.

When you notice these words, it's a sign that you can target both phrases on one page, even if you're just using one of them in your writing. This allows you to target a secondary keyword that shares the same meaning as the primary keyword, even if the actual words aren't the same.

Now that you're an expert at keyphrase research, it's time to learn how to incorporate target phrases into your content.

Writing Headlines: 7-Point Checklist

After years of teaching content marketing, it's time to lay down the law on one of the biggest problems for content marketers: writing headlines.

Headlines are *first impressions*. And you will be judged immediately and ruthlessly by this short set of words.

We all scan (and dismiss) headlines continually. That's what "surfing the web" means. Skimming over waves of headlines.

"The average Internet user sees 1,300+ headlines per day and dismisses 99.7% of them."*

Totally fabricated, but a great headline.

Even if you do everything else right, slaving away in the salt mines of content, working your fingers to the bone, everything will fail if you get this one thing wrong.

So here's how to write a good headline.

This checklist will make sure you've got the right stuff to get the clicks and shares that drive real traffic. And where there's traffic, there's hope.

❏ 1. My Headline Makes a Promise

If you don't explain what's in it for the reader, don't expect them to read it. Period. All great headlines are benefit-driven.

So make a promise. Make it specific.

Ask yourself as if you're the reader. "What's in it for me?" The answer should jump off the page. If it doesn't, be ready to hear crickets. You're about to fail.

In the words of Charlie Meyerson, "Assume your audience isn't interested. Write a headline that spotlights the most compelling, most irresistible part of your content." We'll hear more from Charlie in a minute.

The ability to imagine the readers perspective is the key to success in writing headlines and everything else in your content. *Empathy is the greatest marketing skill.*

Not only do benefit-driven headlines get more clicks, they also get readers to buy. In one A/B test of landing pages by Ion Interactive, the headline that explained the benefits increased conversion rates by 28%. Makes sense.

"Consider content marketing a war zone. The battle is for attention and your headline is your weapon. The reader's perpetually but subconsciously asking, "Why should I read this?" Answer the question. Make it unmistakably clear what the reader gains by investing time in your content.

The pulling power of a magnetic headline traces to its promise. Simply stated, it's a benefit." - **Barry Feldman**, *content marketing consultant and copywriter, Feldman Creative*

❏ 2. My Headline Triggers Curiosity

Specific is good, but don't give everything away. Here's a headline I saw yesterday that I appreciated, but gave me no reason to click.

"Average Full-Time Work Week is 47 Hours, Gallop Says"

That's interesting, but why click? I got the point already.

A great headline triggers curiosity. It doesn't give too much away. Masters of headlines, Buzzfeed and Upworthy, have perfected this craft. Here are some some of Upworthy's most shared headlines, each of which got millions of visits.

- 9 Out of 10 Americans Are Completely Wrong About This Mind-Blowing Fact

- A Brave Fan Asks Patrick Stewart a Question He Doesn't Usually Get and Is Given a Beautiful Answer

- His First 4 Sentences Were Interesting. The 5th Blew My Mind.

- 13 Things You Never Knew About Tequila

- Watch the First 54 Seconds. After That You'll Be Hooked. I Swear.

Teased? That's the idea. You have to click to find out what they're talking about.

These websites pay their bills off the revenue they make from native advertising. So of course, their native advertisers are using the same tricks. To prove the point, take a look at the Native Advertising Leaderboard and you'll see how many of the top native ad headlines create that curiosity gap.

"The [curiosity gap] technique can easily be overdone -- we see brands try to replicate it (badly) all the time. But done right, the so-called curiosity-gap approach can inspire and inform and help readers by making it clear what a piece is about.

The key is to keep yourself honest and use such headlines only when they are helpful triggers for your audience. So go ahead and use "14 Surprising Ways You Can Grow Pumpkins," but only if the 14 ways might indeed be surprising to your audience.

In the same vein, "14 Different Pumpkin Plants That Will Grow in Ridiculously Small Containers" will work only if the said containers actually are, well, ridiculously small." - **Ann Handley**, *Chief Content Officer, Marketing Profs, Author of "Content Rules" and "Everybody Writes"*

❏ 3. My Headline Uses Numbers

List posts are popular for a reason: they set expectations about how much you're getting yourself into. They also suggest variety; if you don't like one thing, you might like something else.

Numerals, not just numbers, are part of the magic. In a line of letters, numerals stand out. So don't write a headline with "Eight Things," write one with "8 things."

A study by Conductor tested five types of headlines. Headlines with numbers won, hands down.

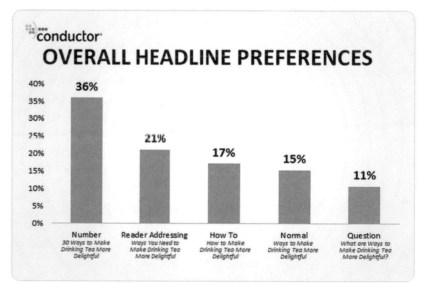

Headlines with numbers aren't always list posts. Numbers can also be data, indicating that the article is supported by research.

Examples:

- 17 Social Media Books That Will Make You a Smarter Marketer
- How to Increase Conversion Rates by 529%
- 101 Ways to Write Top 10 Lists that Increase Traffic By 21%

You get the idea.

"Don't buy the argument that "those headline formulas don't work any more" All that old "cheesy" advice can still be remarkably effective. Make sure there's a benefit to the reader in the headline -- something that person will get out of reading the content. Numbers in the headline still work. List posts still work.

The secret to staying out of Cheeseland? Make the content *behind* your headline amazing. Put some love (and work) into it, to make it compelling and genuinely useful. Bring your own unique writing voice and sincere care for the topic into your written, audio, and video content." - **Sonia Simone**, *Chief Marketing Officer, Copyblogger*

❏ 4. My Headline Asks a Question

Question headlines have two benefits. First, they leverage a psychological effect, causing the reader's mind to take the next step: answer the question ...or wonder. The lack of completeness inherent in questions causes tension and interest in readers.

Search is the second benefit. Google is focused on the meaning of a search query, not just combinations of words. It's called "semantic indexing." The natural language of a complete question helps Google understand how the article is useful.

People are using their voices, not just fingers, to search these days. This is part of the trend toward mobile. Naturally, they're asking complete, full-sentence questions.

Complete questions and complete answers will help Google connect people to your content. Question headlines help future-proof your content for SEO.

Examples:

- Why Do Dogs Bark at Night? 5 Dog Trainers Offer Tips for Quiet Canines.
- Which Superhero Are You? Take this short quiz and find out….
- How Does Social Media Affect SEO? (this was a recent post/video on this blog)

"The power of question headlines comes from tapping into what keeps your readers up at night. Increase your question title's effectiveness by making it personal. Include the word "you."

The drawback of question titles is that its open-ended nature looses some clarity. This can hinder title performance. Therefore, when I use a question title, I use the subtitle to clarify any open points." - **Heidi Cohen**, *Actionable Marketing Guide*

❏ 5. My Headline Uses Power Words

Some words get clicked more than others. Other words get shared more. Word choice is critical to writing headlines. So choose carefully.

Luckily, there's data on which words get the best results. Here's a summary of research on the power words.

- Words that get more clicks from search results: *How to, [List-related numbers], Free, You, Tips, Blog post, Why, Best, Tricks, Great*

- Words that get shared more (appear most often in viral posts): *Smart, Surprising, Science, History, Hacks (hacking, hackers and "life hack" related topics), Huge / Big, Critical*

- Negative words that get shared more (negative words from viral posts): *Kill, Fear, Dark, Bleeding, War*

- Words that get retweeted more: *You, Twitter, Please, Retweet, Post, Blog, Social, Free, Media, Help*

- Words that increase email open rates: *Urgent, Breaking, Important, Alert*

To see the research behind these recommendations, I wrote an article about it called 131 words that increase website traffic.

Notice any patterns? Some of these are from earlier points on the checklist. The word 'You' appears several times. If you've written a benefit-driven headline, you've probably covered this already.

"Every headline needs to offer a promise that the body copy delivers on. I don't know about you, but I like my promises to be more than vanilla. They need to sound like amazing opportunities. Otherwise, they're not much of a promise. The way to capture attention is to employ powerful words in your headline that get the reader excited to read the whole article."
- **Jeff Goins**, *Goins, Writer*

❏ **6. My Headline Is Sized to Fit Its Purpose**

Length matters. But different sizes fit different places. Headlines are everywhere, but they're not one-size-fits-all. Here are places where your headline is likely to appear.

- **Email Subject Lines** in the inbox
- **Posts and Tweets** in social streams
- **Search Results Pages** from your <title> tag
- **At the top of the page** in the header <h1> tag

You don't have to use the same headline in every location. Pro marketers will tailor the length to the location, writing different headlines for different places. Here's a guide for "headline" length.

Ideal Length for "Headlines" in various places	
Title tags	55 characters
Email subject lines (for open rates)	50 characters or less
Facebook post (for likes & shares)	100-140 characters
Tweets (for retweets)	120-130 characters

To learn more about the logic and research behind these recommendations, take a look at this post: *The Ideal Length for Everything In Your Marketing.*

"Place the story's most interesting word or phrase as close as possible to the start of the headline. This becomes even more crucial as people read on their smartphones, where email subject lines can get truncated to 3 or 4 words." - **Charlie Meyerson**, *Principal, Meyerson Strategy (and news media veteran of 14 years)*

❏ 7. My Headline Puts the Keyword First

Using the target keyphrase at the beginning of the headline gives you good "keyphrase prominence" helping to indicate relevance to search engines.

It's especially important for both the title tag <title> and the header <h1>. This is fundamental to on-page SEO best practices. It's not important for email subject lines and social media post headlines.

This may come naturally when you target longer, less competitive "how to" or question phrases. It's more difficult when writing those Upworthy-style curiosity gap headlines.

Conflicted? Yes, some of these tips contradict others. So here's a pro-tip you probably haven't seen before. This is part of our secret writing sauce here at Orbit…

PRO-TIP!: *Combine Search-Friendly and Social-Friendly Headlines*: To create headlines that rank in search engines and get traction with readers, use a colon. This lets you separate the search-friendly keyword from the social-friendly click bait.

It's a way to get good keyphrase prominence but still leverage human psychology in the rest of the headline.

Check out these *examples* from our past posts on orbitmedia.com/blog:

- How to Research Keywords: Tips, Competition and Squirrels
- Competitive Analysis Tools: 5 Free Ways to See the Analytics of Any Website
- Neuromarketing Web Design: 15 Ways to Connect with Visitors' Brains
- Internal Linking: 9 Best Practices for Internal Links
- Ego Bait: 5 Simple Ways to Leverage Blog Mentions
- Thank You Pages: 9 Example of Missed Opportunities

See the pattern? Each post is optimized to rank for the phrase at the beginning of the headline (with perfect keyphrase prominence) followed by a number or words to connect with visitors' hearts and minds.

So here's Orbit's formula for headlines:

Target Keyphrase + Colon + Number or Trigger Word + Promise

Does it work? Search for any of those phrases before the colon. You probably see the post ranking for the phrase …and you might just click, thanks to the numbers and curiosity gaps.

Bonus Tips (and Promises Kept)

This is a huge and important topic. We didn't cover everything here. These tips didn't make the checklist but this wouldn't be complete without them.

- **Write LOTS of headlines before choosing one:** We write dozens before choosing one for an article.
- **Write headlines that create some urgency:** Hurry up and do this before your competition does!
- **Check the "Emotional Value" of your headline:** Put your headline into Advanced Marketing Institute's Headline Analyzer, which will give you a percentage score of the emotional value. The higher, the better.

- **Add a fun theme, then share with specific people:** Adding a theme adds interest. If you write a zombie-themed article about search marketing, you can then find people who love zombies and SEO. There are 31 people with "zombie" and "SEO" in their Twitter bios.

  Learn how exactly to do this here: Sharing Content with Laser Focus.

- **KEEP YOUR PROMISES:** If the headline doesn't fit the article, don't use it or you'll erode trust with your readers. That "ultimate guide" had better be the best. Those "5 Easy Ways" better not be complicated!

Article checklist

Before you click the publish button, make sure you've included these properties and that you're doing them all in the right way. Incorporating them into your content will make the next step, content promotion, far easier and more effective.

	Properties
Title	❏ Includes the target keyphrase once, at the beginning of the title if possible. ❏ Max 55 characters
Meta description	❏ Includes the target keyphrase ❏ Max 155 characters
Keyphrase usage	❏ Keyphrase used four to six times in the article
Formatting	❏ Headers and subheads ❏ Short paragraphs ❏ Bullet lists
Links	❏ Link to product or service page ❏ Links to related posts or pages (optional)
Images	❏ Minimum one image (copyright and possibly attribution)
Mention	❏ Mentions: Experts and/or someone active on social media (optional)
Call to action	❏ Invites reader to comment, subscribe, etc.
Length	❏ 1500 words for search optimized posts and pages
Author box	❏ Several sentences about the author's relevance ❏ Link to full on-site bio or Google+ profile ❏ Link to Twitter and LinkedIn accounts

Title: It's the text at the top of the browser, above the address bar, for any web page. Depending on your browser, it may also be in the tab. In the code, it's whatever text is inside the <title> tags. It is very important.

The title becomes the link when the page or post ranks in search engines. If it's too long, it gets truncated. 55 characters is the limit. Be brief.

Titles are strong indicators to search engines of what the page is about, so use your target keyphrase, use it once, and if possible, use it at the beginning of the title. The prominence of the keyphrase (in other words, how close it appears to the beginning) is very important.

It might be tempting to put your business name at the front of the title. Don't. Search engine marketers have a saying: "*Brand last.*" Start with your keyphrase, end with your business name. Remember, your first goal is to help people. Promoting yourself comes second.

Fig. 16

Chicago Ecommerce Web Design & Development | Orbit ...
www.orbitmedia.com/**ecommerce-web-design** ▾ Orbit Media Studios ▾
Orbit has **designed** and built hundreds of **e-commerce websites** since 2001, for
companies around the country and here in **Chicago**. **E-commerce** sites need to ...

◀━━━ **LINK:** tilte of the page

◀━━━ **SNIPPET:** meta decription
of the page (or occasionally,
a page excerpt)

Meta Description: Although meta keywords are almost totally useless, the Meta Description remains important. It doesn't appear in the content of the page, but it is highly visible in search results. Below each link in a search results page is a "snippet" of text. In Google this snippet is either an excerpt from the body text or, more often, the meta description. So make it good.

Write it as a single-sentence, plain English summary of the content. Don't just use the title or headline. Use your target keyphrase at least once, but not more than twice. Limit the number of characters to 155 to be sure the description will fit within the snippet. *(fig. 16)*

📝 **NOTE!** *Rich snippets:* Big changes in Google are leading to much more interesting snippets. You might have already noticed movie times and product reviews appearing as snippets. These are called "rich snippets" and are possible when specific tags are added to page elements. They may include reviews when product pages rank, ingredients when recipe pages rank, and movie times when your local theater ranks. Google is gradually adding all kinds of information to search results pages.

Keyphrase Usage: We recommend including the target keyphrase in the body of the article at least twice, but not more than five times. In each instance, all the words in the phrase should appear together as a "bonded" phrase. This should come naturally if the phrase is relevant to the topic. During editing, go back to make sure it's used but not overused.

💡 **TIP!** It's likely that punctuation is dropped in Google, so if you're having trouble incorporating the phrase, consider ending one sentence with the beginning of the phrase, and beginning the next sentence with the end of the phrase. For example, if you're targeting "Tampa telephone repair," the following sentences include one instance of the phrase:

We're located in north **Tampa.**
Telephone repair services include dial tone tuning and button replacement.

⚠️ **CAUTION!** Don't overdo it on the keyphrase usage. If you compromise your writing to the extent that it makes no sense to your human reader, you're probably guilty of "keyword stuffing." Using the phrase over and over in unnatural ways is both terrible for your readers and bad for search engine optimization. Google can see right through this and there's a chance you'll be penalized. So don't do it!

Formatting: People tend not to read online; we tend to scan. Content marketers must accept this and adapt by adding formatting to their content. Big, blocky, dense paragraphs are less likely to be read. Content with more formatting is more likely to engage the reader.

- **Headers and subheads**: Breaking up the article into short sections makes it much more accessible to busy readers. Each section should begin with a header that serves as a mini headline for the paragraphs that follow.

- **Short paragraphs**: Generally, no paragraph should include more than three or four lines. Very short paragraphs of one sentence or even one word can be used to add emphasis.

- **Bullet lists and numbered lists**: These are very easy to scan and work well within almost any post. Some very successful posts are nothing more than lists. Some blogs, such as 12most.com, are based entirely on list formatted content.

- **Bold and italics**: Excellent ways to add emphasis and make content more easily scanned, but don't overdo it.

Formatting is good for search engines as well as humans. If you leave out the formatting, you miss opportunities to use your keyphrase in more ways. Subheaders and bullet lists are opportunities to use words from a target phrase and indicate relevance a bit more.

Links: Your goal as a content marketer is to eventually convert visitors into leads and customers. As Barry Feldman put it, "Your site is the mousetrap, your content is the cheese." If you don't help make those connections between the cheese and the trap, you catch fewer mice.

Look for opportunities within articles to link to web pages about your products and services, and to other content. Doing so creates a benefit for conversions and a visible impact on the "average pages per visit" metric in Analytics.

There is also an SEO benefit to this. Internal linking is an easy opportunity to use keyphrases within the link text. When linking to other content, use the target keyphrase in the links. Although these links have far less impact on rank than links from other websites, they are still helpful in indicating relevance to search engines.

Example: Consider which of the two following links does a better job of indicating relevance:

1. Learn more about <u>hedgehog shampoo</u>.

2. <u>Click here</u> to learn more about hedgehog shampoo.

The first example tells the search engines what's behind the click and what the subsequent page is about. The second example does not.

💡 **TIP!** Every few months, go back and look at older posts. Try to find opportunities to add links to your more recent content and vice versa.

Images: Posts with images are more interesting to look at and more likely to be shared. Some posts are dominated by images. A post called "10 Great Uses of Typography on Home Pages" may consist mostly of screenshots. These types of posts are often very successful in social media.

Infographics are another great example. They are nothing more than a giant image with little or no text surrounding the image on the page. And they frequently go viral. Infographics are typically highly visual representations of data and statistics, but often they are simply cleverly reformatted lists.

The following infographic is a list of the relative effectiveness of various SEO link building strategies, formatted to look like a popular board game. Brilliant!

Adding images to posts is also important because when content is shared in social networks, an image from the page is generally pulled in and appears within the post. This makes the content more prominent in that social stream. Shared posts without images are not as prominent and have a visual disadvantage.

Some sites have a policy of never publishing a post without at least one image. If you guest post on these sites, they may reject your post unless you add an image, or they may add images for you. They may use a lot of bad stock photos and it might not be pretty. Plan ahead and find an image at a site like http://www.istockphoto.com/ or http://www.flickr.com/creativecommons/.

Mentions: Don't hesitate to mention other people within your content. Input from experts adds credibility and makes your content more interesting. For promotional reasons, it can be effective to deliberately mention those who are active in social media. They may share your content once it's posted.

Some content was made to be shared. Here are some examples:

- Event recap: Short event summary that mentions attendees and presenters.

- Ask the Experts: Send a few questions to five or more experts.

- Response articles: Refer to something recently published. Act quickly to make it part of the conversation.

In each case, the article is likely to be shared by the people you mentioned. It's useful to mention those who have social followings.

Source: linkbuilding.nl

Call to Action: Now that you have provided friendly, helpful advice to your readers, it's time to ask for a little bit in return. Every great post has a call to action that invites the visitor to become more engaged with your content or your business.

For blog posts, the call to action might simply be an *invitation to leave a comment*. Ask a question that the reader can answer with a comment, solicit other ideas that would complement the suggestions made in the post or even invite the reader to disagree with you.

Beyond comments, a call to action may be a one-sentence pitch to subscribe to the newsletter. If the content was truly useful, the moment they finish reading the post is the high point of their appreciation and the most likely time for readers to subscribe.

For web pages, a call to action may be a link directing visitors to read more on another page. Or best of all, it's an offer to start a conversation. The call to action could be a polite invitation to fill out a short form...and become a lead.

TIP! Calls to action should use the same compelling language that you use while authoring subject lines, headers, Tweets and anything else that you want a reader to act on. "Contact us" is not a call to action. "Ask Andy for more advice on web marketing" is.

Length: Whenever possible, use short paragraphs, short sentences and short words. But don't worry about writing short articles. Each piece of content should be as long as it needs to be to convey the meaning and not a word longer.

> "Data shows that posts with images get more views, shares, and time on page. There's something about making content visually interesting that **gets people to bounce less**."
>
> SHANE SNOW, CO-FOUNDER, CONTENTLY

Inspired? Explaining a complex idea? Giving detailed instructions? Pay no attention to length. Just keep writing in clear, concise language until you're done. For detailed guidelines on the ideal length for everything in your marketing, see below.

TIP! It's also important to use simple language. In a study by the NN Group, a healthcare website was rewritten to bring down the readability level in an attempt to improve the success rate for visitors. They discovered that eighth-grade level writing improved results for all visitors, not just those with lower literacy skills.

Sucess Rate	Original Site	Rewritten Site
Lower-literacy users	46%	82%
Higher-literacy users	68%	93%

Even PhDs prefer to read at an eighth-grade level.

A Few Words about Length

What is the ideal length for your content? "It depends." What a totally unsatisfying answer. Of course it depends. But there are rules of thumb. There is research. We can analyze what works and draw conclusions. We can create guidelines, especially for things that are measurable. Like length.

Here are length guidelines for ten types of content. Most of these are compiled from studies that analyzed the high performers. Take a look:

Ideal Length Guidelines for Everything in Your Marketing	
Blog posts (for ranking)	1,500 words
Email subject lines (for open rates)	50 characters or less
Line of text	12 words
Paragraph	4 lines or less
YouTube video (for views)	3 - 3.5 minutes
Podcast	22 minutes
Title tags	55 characters (maximum)
Meta descriptions	155 characters (maximum)
Facebook post (for likes and shares)	100 - 140 characters
Tweet (for retweets)	120 - 130 characters

Now that you've got the data, let's look at the research...

Ideal Blog Post Length for SEO

Blog posts vary in length from a few short paragraphs (Seth Godin style) to 40,000 words (Neil Patel style). If your goal is search engine traffic, longer is better.

When serpIQ analyzed high ranking pages, they found more text correlates with high rankings. *(fig. 18a)*

On this chart, "content" includes navigation, sidebar content, and other page elements, so the numbers here look slightly higher than the recommended blog post length.

Think about it this way: Google is a research tool. Longer pages have more opportunities to indicate their relevance. Google sees longer pages as more likely to contain the answer to the searcher's question.

Another reason is links. When MOZ analyzed 3,800 posts on their own blog, they found that the longer posts get linked to more often. Longer pages generally attract more links, and these links support a higher rank.

The ideal length for a search-optimized blog post is 1,500 words.

Ideal Length for an Email Subject Line

Surprisingly, the length of an email subject line doesn't have a big impact on open and clickthrough rates. According to a study by MailChimp, shorter subject lines perform only slightly better. *(fig. 18b)*

Even if the benefits are in the single digits, most experts would say shorter is better. Especially for mobile recipients—longer subject lines get truncated when viewed on a phone.

The ideal email subject line is 50 characters or less.

Ideal Line Length

It's all in the biology of the human eye.

According to the Web Style Guide, the field of vision for readers is only a few inches. If a line of text is too long, the reader needs to use more muscles in the eye and neck. It takes more work to travel all the way across a long line of text, back and forth, over and over. Readers are more likely to lose their place. This slows reading rates and comprehension.

The length of a line of text is typically determined during the web design process, so if you want to change it, you may need to have your web designer tweak your CSS files.

The ideal length for a line of text is 12 words.

Ideal Paragraph Length

When you open a book, you expect to hit a wall of text. But books don't have back buttons. On the web, long paragraphs are a problem.

Website visitors are often scanners. Short paragraphs let them get the meaning in short bursts. Many (even most) visitors scan down the page, glancing at headers and sub-headers, then dive deeper into the paragraphs if something catches their interest.

Fig. 18a

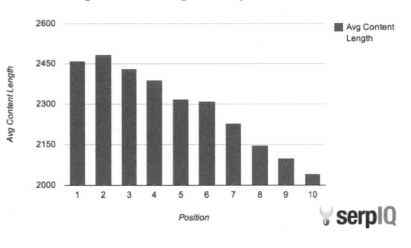

Fig. 18b

Subject Line Character Count vs. Open Rate

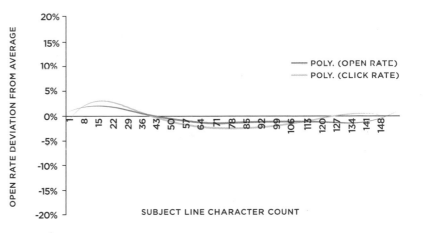

"Short paragraphs get read, long paragraphs get skimmed, really long paragraphs get skipped." -**Jason Fried**

Designers know that visitors love whitespace, but somehow, writers didn't get the message. Don't write walls of text. Break up paragraphs to create whitespace on the page.

The ideal length for a paragraph is 3 to 4 lines maximum.

Ideal Length for a YouTube Video

Some YouTube videos are hundreds of hours long...but they're not very popular. The most popular videos are pretty short.

When David Waterhouse analyzed the length of the top 50 YouTube videos, he found the average length was 2 minutes 54 seconds. Clinton Stark reported that Google researchers from the YouTube team confirmed this recommended length.

Website visitors are often scanners. Short paragraphs let them get the meaning in short bursts.

Why are short videos popular on YouTube? Consider this:

- YouTube is the second most popular search engine in the world
- The percentage of viewers who watched the entire video is a ranking factor

So if it's very long, fewer viewers may watch the entire video, which could cause it to rank lower, be discovered less often and be less popular.

The ideal length for a YouTube video is 3 to 3½ minutes.

Ideal Length for a Podcast

The length of podcasts ranges almost as much as YouTube videos. Some popular podcasts are 60 seconds; others are several hours. The top 10 business podcasts range from 15 minutes to an hour, averaging 42 minutes.

According to research by Stitcher, the typical podcast listener stays connected for 22 minutes on average.

This number isn't surprising. Studies cited in the National Teaching and Learning Forum show that students zone out after 15-20 minutes of lecture time. After 20 minutes, attention and retention rates crash.

The ideal length for a podcast is 22 minutes.

Ideal Length for a Title Tag

Besides the blog post itself, there are a few other parts of the page that affect SEO. The most important of these is the title tag. Why so important? The title tag becomes the link when the page ranks in Google.

According to recent research by Dr. Pete over at Moz, the title tag guidelines have changed due to the redesign of Google's search results. Using the new title tag preview tool, this is what your title tag will look like: *(fig. 18c)*

If a title is too long, it gets truncated, and people won't be able to read it all. The cutoff point is around 60 characters. So use the target keyphrase once and keep it short. See Orbit's SEO Best Practices for more info.

The ideal length for a title tag is 55 characters.

Ideal Length for Meta Description

As with the title tag, the meta description is visible in search results, and it gets cut off if it's too long. *(fig. 18d)*

It should be a single sentence in plain English, summarizing the content of the page. Use the target keyphrase once and don't make it too long.

The ideal length for a meta description is 155 characters.

Ideal Length of a Facebook Post

According to research by Track Social, shorter Facebook messages get more engagement. Here's the correlation between length and likes: *(fig. 18e)*

Length isn't the only factor, or even the most important factor; Facebook posts with images get four times as much response

Enter Your Full Title Text:

Chicago Web Design and Development Company

Enter Search Phrase *(optional)*:

chicago web design

Cutts Me, Google!

Chicago Web Design and Development Company
www.example.com/example
This is your page description. The font and size of the description has not changed in the latest redesign. Descriptions get cut off after roughly 160 characters ...

Orbit Media: **Chicago Web Design** and Development Company
www.orbitmedia.com/ ▾
Orbit Media is a **Chicago web design** and development firm, creating custom, clean and effective websites since 2001.
Blog - Custom Web Design - Contact - Careers

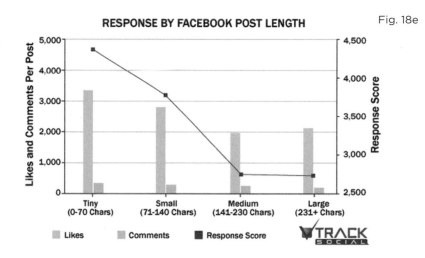

RESPONSE BY FACEBOOK POST LENGTH

as posts without. But, if a Facebook post is longer than the longest Tweet (140 characters), response rates drop off fast.

The ideal length for a Facebook post is 100 to 140 characters.

Ideal Length of a Tweet

So, if Facebook posts should be as long as Tweets, then 140 characters is a good length, right? Actually, that might not be true.

Dan Zarrella of HubSpot analyzed 200,000 Tweets with links to see if length correlated with high clickthrough rates. It does. Longer Tweets tend to get more clicks, but the maximum 140 characters wasn't the highest. The peak looks to be around 120 to 130 characters: *(fig. 18f)*

The ideal length for a Tweet is 120 to 130 characters.

Fig. 18f

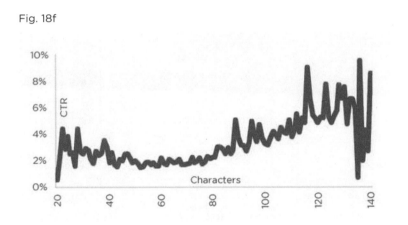

The Ultimate Rule for Content Length

These are guidelines, not rules. Making it longer or shorter doesn't guarantee failure; making it exactly these lengths doesn't guarantee success. Even this post and it's corresponding email didn't follow each guideline exactly!

There's really only one hard, fast rule for content length and it goes like this:

Every piece of content should be as long as it takes to convey the message, and no longer.

Sample Article

The following article includes all the properties that make up a good piece of web content. An edited version of this article ran as a guest post on Marketing Profs on April 12, 2012.

This is a good web marketing article: 7 reasons

Rather than just describing best practices for a web marketing article, let's wrap them all together in a self-referential post. It's so meta! Here are the seven reasons why this is a good web marketing article.

1. This article is optimized for search engines.
Before I started writing, I looked at Google AdWords Keyword Planner and discovered that 320 people search for "web marketing article" each month. So I decided to do a little SEO copywriting and included the phrase once in the title, once in the URL and six times in the body of the article itself.

It's kind of a competitive phrase, but why not give it a shot? It doesn't take long. So this article is search optimized.

2. This article has an image.
Articles with images are more likely to be shared, so I'm putting in an image. Here it is:

Articles with images look good, partly because when they're shared in social networks (Facebook, Google+, LinkedIn, etc.) a thumbnail of the image appears.

Dr David Jefferies, Guildford, Surrey UK

This article is about itself. So is this image... and this sentence.

3. This article mentions other people and blogs.

If you mention people in your posts, you might get their attention, and they just might share it through their networks. Copyblogger actually gives three reasons for this: credibility, promotion and networking.

Simply put, one of the fastest ways to grow a new blog is to mention other sites with big audiences in your guest post appearances.

If you drop a handy email or Tweet before the guest post goes live, you can harness the sheer awesomeness of their contact lists. Most of the time they will at least Tweet out your guest post and thus associate themselves with your content.

So mention a big blog and let them know about the post...just like that!

4. This article has lots of formatting.

A web marketing article should have plenty of formatting, making it scannable for visitors. Formatting makes articles much easier for visitors to read and a bit easier for search engines to rank. This article uses:

- Headers and subheaders
- Short paragraphs (no paragraph is longer than three sentences)
- Bullet lists, like this one

5. This article links to another page or post.

A good web marketer always looks for opportunities for internal linking. These links are an important part of *web strategy*. This is a good web marketing article, partly because of the link. The link is good for two reasons:

- It tells Google that the page you're linking to is relevant for the phrase within the link.
- It guides visitors from one page to the next through a "conversion funnel." Links pull visitors deeper into the site, toward the contact form, where they may become a lead.

6. This article doesn't take itself too seriously.

If it did, it wouldn't have been much fun to write and it probably would be no fun to read. This is web marketing, not a bone marrow transplant.

7. This article has a call to action for comments.

Here goes: If you can think of anything that would make this a great web marketing article, I would love to hear suggestions. Feel free to leave a comment below. I'm always learning and interested in any feedback.

Andy Crestodina is the strategic director of Orbit Media, a web development company in Chicago. You can find Andy on Google+ and Twitter.

Content Quality

Content chemistry is a science, but don't forget the art. If your writing is boring, salesy or irrelevant, no amount of chemistry will help. All the usual rules apply. Know your audience. Do your research. Tell a story. Find your voice.

These are all critically important, but they are not our focus here. Still, I can share with you a general structure and approach for writing, after the planning and research are complete. We're going to reconstruct a popular post from the Orbit Media Blog called Your Brand is Your Blog, Your Blog is Your Brand, originally written by our very own Mary Fran Wiley.

1. Write the "takeaway," a single sentence summary.

First, Mary Fran determined the overall point of her post:

You have to identify the voice of your brand; you need to figure out who the voice behind the blog is and to whom it is speaking.

2. Write the outline and headers.

Then Mary Fran laid out the main points she wanted to make, in the order she wanted to make them:

Your Brand is Your Blog, Your Blog is Your Brand

1. Start by carving your niche.

2. Embrace your personality (or your brand's personality).

3. Go ahead, get out there and shine!

3. Fill in the blanks with short, rough paragraphs.

Next, she added bullet points under the main points, then went back and added a sentence or two to explain each bullet point:

Your Brand is Your Blog, Your Blog is Your Brand

1. Start by carving your niche.
Be different.
Be awesome at just one thing.
Always be improving.

2. Embrace your personality
(or your brand's personality).
Put yourself out there.
Share your opinions and views.
Be consistent.

3. Go ahead, get out there and shine!
Join the conversation.
Connect with people.
Be humble.

4. Edit, refine and polish.

And finally, Mary Fran spent some time editing and revising the post, and asked a few colleagues to proofread it for her before it was published.

See Mary Fran's completed post on the Orbit Media Blog: *Your Brand Is Your Blog, Your Blog Is Your Brand.*

Content criteria: Don't publish unless you meet one of these 3 criteria.

I read a lot of blogs—some good, some bad. A few weeks ago, I read something by Bill Sebald that stuck with me. He said:

I urge you to start writing content that actually is either 1) actionable, 2) a strong opinion, or 3) proven to some degree.

These are great blog criteria. Basically, if it's not useful, if it's a weak opinion or if it makes unsupported claims, it's probably not good. This makes sense.

Then I came across something in a book called *Elements of Content Strategy* by Erin Kissane. Erin explains how good content works by relating to the context of the reader. There are three elements: physical (doing), emotional (feeling) and cognitive (learning). *(fig 19)*

Fig. 19

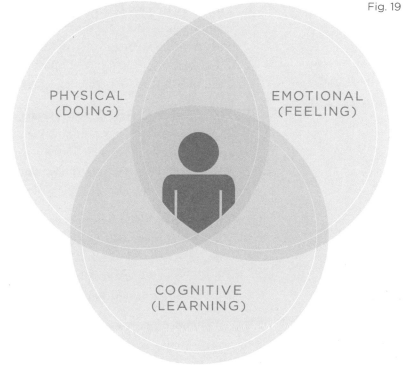

PHYSICAL
(DOING)

EMOTIONAL
(FEELING)

COGNITIVE
(LEARNING)

Sound familiar? The three blogging criteria recommended by Sebald align perfectly with the user contexts described by Kissane.

- **Actionable = Physical**
- **Proven = Cognitive**
- **Strong Opinion = Emotional**

Unless the post connects on one of these levels, it probably isn't worth the reader's time (and they're certainly not going to share it). We all need to make sure that our content meets one or more of these three criteria:

1. **The reader can DO something.** It's practical. There are steps they can take. Actionable posts lend themselves to list formats, which makes a post more scannable and reader-friendly.

2. **The reader LEARNS something.** If you want to teach something, you need supporting evidence. Facts, research and expert input make your assertions more believable.

3. **The reader FEELS something.** You felt something while you wrote it. It's your voice and your opinion. It means something to you, good or bad. If you don't care, why would your readers?

If your content doesn't meet at least one of these criteria for writing, try one of these tips:

Give instructions: Step-by-step instructions (like this section), lists of action items and how-to posts are extremely popular for a good reason: the goal is to help the reader.

Add examples: If you make assertions but don't give examples, you may be making unsupported claims. This is why Harvard Business School focuses on case studies. Without proof, it's just academic. Add examples, surveys, statistics, quotes, screenshots and any other supportive content.

Add some attitude: Don't hedge your bets. Edit that first draft and take out all those qualifying words. They take the directness and edge out of your writing. During editing you can tweak the tone and strengthen opinions. Do it right and a group of sentences like this:

> "In many cases, blog posts are vague and may not be useful to readers. This is often because they do not provide enough actionable advice."

...becomes a sentence like this:

> "Vague blog posts aren't useful, since they just aren't actionable for readers."

...or even this:

> "If a blog post isn't actionable, it's useless."

A few words about quality...

There are hundreds of books and thousands of blog posts about writing great content. Many of these were written by true masters of the craft. Here are a few quotes from some of the greats. These should give you a bit more insight and maybe even some inspiration.

"On the average, five times as many people read the headline as read the body copy. When you have written your headline, you have spent eighty cents out of your dollar." -**David Ogilvy**

"Clarity trumps persuasion"
-**Dr. Flint McGlaughlin**

"Make the customer the hero of your story" -**Ann Handley**

"Stop trying to write. Do more research." -**Robert Bruce**

"Copy is never written. Copy is assembled." -**Eugene Schwartz**

"Write a crappy first draft."
-**Brad Farris**

"The more informative your advertising, the more persuasive it will be." -**David Ogilvy**

"Be a person." -**Sonia Simone**

"The difference between the almost right word and the right word is really a large matter—it's the difference between the lightning bug and the lightning." -**Mark Twain**

"In this age of microblogging and two-second sound bites, almost no one has the attention span, or time, to read more than a few sentences." -**Tim Frick**

"Focus on the core problem your business solves and put out lots of content and enthusiasm, and ideas about how to solve that problem."
-**Laura Fitton**

"The **more informative** your advertising, the **more persuasive** it will be."

DAVID OGILVY

"Authenticity, honesty, and personal voice underlie much of what's successful on the Web." -**Rick Levine**

"I urge you to start writing content that actually is either 1) actionable, 2) a strong opinion, or 3) proven to some degree." -**Bill Sebald**

"Remarkable social media content and great sales copy are pretty much the same - plain spoken words designed to focus on the needs of the reader, listener or viewer." -**Brian Clark**

"Don't bunt. Aim out of the ball park. Aim for the company of immortals."
-**David Ogilvy**

"The secret to prolifically creating excellent content isn't inspiration or brilliance—it's found in structure, planning and research. Start with the audience and the angle." - **Danny Iny**

That last quote is from an excellent post by Danny Iny on Copyblogger: *A Fool-Proof Formula for Creating Compelling Content.*

Content Hubs

Online competition is intense. Close to *2 million blog posts are published* every day. That's a lot of content. A bit discouraging, isn't it?

But take a moment to think about the nature of competition. Online competition is based on topics. In Google, in social media, and in the minds of your audience, competition for attention is always specific to a topic.

Popular topics are crowded with competitors: famous blogs, big companies, and sites that have invested in content for years. If the topic is small, small websites can win attention, but it may not be enough to generate leads and sales. It's hard to thrive in a tiny, micro-niche. *(fig. 20)*

Fig. 20

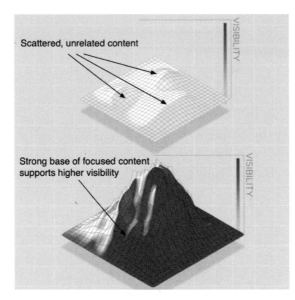

So How Do You Beat the Competition For Bigger Topics?

First, you have to understand this: those bigger competitors win because they have more content and better content. This is

how they become relevant for that topic in search engines, in social media, and with their email subscribers.

So to compete, you need to focus on a topic and build up a set of content around it. You need to be more organized and focused. To beat the big boys, you need content hubs.

When content is focused on a topic, it piles up, reaching higher above the competition and gaining visibility. If a content hub were drawn in 3D, *it would look like a mountain*, with a central peak surrounded by a wide base of sub-topics.

Most marketers aren't very focused. They publish a bit here and there. These are just small hills that never rise high enough to be visible.

So What's a Content Hub?

A content hub is a set of content (usually web pages) organized around a specific topic (usually a central page). It could be a category on a blog or a section of pages on a website. So content hubs are relevant to both web design and ongoing content marketing.

Sitemaps: Website sections are content hubs for related services. Ecommerce product catalogs often resemble content hubs. Make sure to use descriptive navigation and pay close attention to internal linking. See How to Make a Sitemap for details.

Blogs: Blog categories can be topic-based and often serve as content hubs.

Content Strategy: A publishing calendar can focus on a specific topic for a specific time frame.

Content hubs are the key to winning attention in a crowded field. They work because they have a structure: a wide base around a high center.

DON'T: Build a pile of medium quality blog posts that all say similar things.

DO: Create a well organized hub of diverse assets, in many formats, in many places, created by various people.

- **Content on interrelated topics:** The posts or pages support each other, inviting the visitor to dig deeper through internal links, like a mini-Wikipedia. *(fig. 21a)*

- **Content targeted related phrases:** The center of the hub targets the broadest, most popular but most competitive keyphrase. It it supported by many pages that target related phrases, forming a large set of interconnected keyphrase-focused pages. *(fig. 21b)*

- **Content in different formats:** "What" you publish should vary. Appeal to your audiences' various learning styles using different formats: blog posts, guides, videos, infographics, audio, etc. *(fig. 21c)*

- **Content on other websites:** "Where" you publish should also vary. Write for other publications. *(fig. 21d)*

- **Content created together with influencers:** "Who" creates this content? You don't have to do all the work. Co-create content with people your audience trusts, people who have already built an audience that overlaps with yours. Collaborate with influencers *(fig. 21e)*.

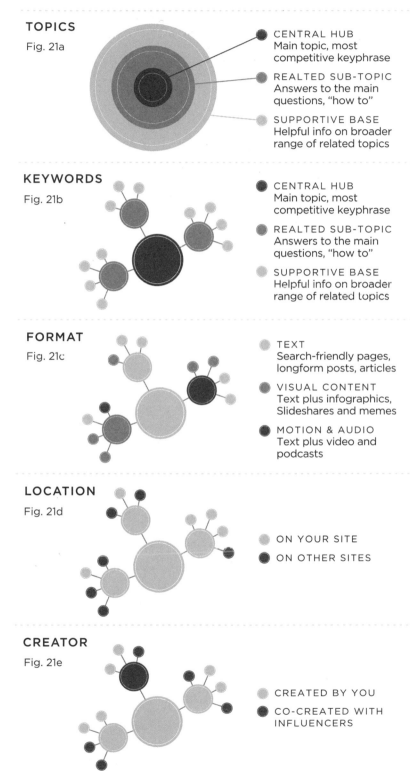

CONTENT HUB STRUCTURE:

TOPICS
Fig. 21a

CENTRAL HUB
Main topic, most competitive keyphrase

REALTED SUB-TOPIC
Answers to the main questions, "how to"

SUPPORTIVE BASE
Helpful info on broader range of related topics

KEYWORDS
Fig. 21b

CENTRAL HUB
Main topic, most competitive keyphrase

REALTED SUB-TOPIC
Answers to the main questions, "how to"

SUPPORTIVE BASE
Helpful info on broader range of related topics

FORMAT
Fig. 21c

TEXT
Search-friendly pages, longform posts, articles

VISUAL CONTENT
Text plus infographics, Slideshares and memes

MOTION & AUDIO
Text plus video and podcasts

LOCATION
Fig. 21d

ON YOUR SITE
ON OTHER SITES

CREATOR
Fig. 21e

CREATED BY YOU
CO-CREATED WITH INFLUENCERS

How to Create a Content Hub

Here's the fun part. The general idea is to simply create more stuff, focused on a topic, organized around a central hub. But you'll get better results if you take a more strategic approach:

1. Pick a topic that's valuable to you and important to your audience. Think about the questions your content can answer, the problems your business solves, and the phrases your audience is likely to search for. Make a list of these questions, answers and keywords. They should be closely related.

2. Check the competition by searching for the phrases in Google. Use the MozBar to see the domain authority of the high ranking sites. Use Open Site Explorer to check your own domain authority. Normally, you'd need an authority in the high end of the range of the high ranking sites. But since we're building an entire hub of content, we can win even for the more difficult phrases.

3. Find the influencers who are relevant for these topics with your audience. You want to start making friends with these people early in the process. Follow them, share their content, comment and do anything else that slowly wins their attention in a positive way.

4. Publish the central hub. This will be the center of the content hub. Make it your simplest, strongest and most useful piece of content on the topic. Optimize it for the most valuable and competitive keyphrase. Give it a clear call to action.

5. Publish supportive content. Put your best advice out there. Each piece can target its own phrase, which are subtopics of the central hub.

Make sure to create visual content that looks great when shared on social networks. Also, make sure everything links back to your hub. Use the target phrase for the hub in some of the links.

6. Co-create with the influencers who are now in your network. Interview them, ask them for quotes, include them in a survey, poll or research study. Make them aware of the hub you've created and politely request that they share. Invite them to contribute a guest post or offer to write something for their site...

NOTE! Big thanks to *Lee Odden of TopRank Blog* for his clear-sighted presentation about influencer outreach at Social Media Marketing World. Inspiring as always, Lee!

7. Publish on other websites. Pitch related posts to relevant blogs and media sites. These could be alternate versions of content you've published, created through a process of ethical content spinning. In each case, they should link back to the hub.

By the end of the process, you should be able to check Analytics and see if you're winning attention. It will look like a steady stream of search traffic for the related phrases, and small spikes of social traffic each time something is published.

If you're not winning, you're not done yet. Build higher. If you are winning, congratulations! You're relevant for the topic. Now go build another content hub.

Why Do Content Hubs Work?

There are specific reasons why hubs are necessary and effective:

- **Search Benefits: Google's "Hummingbird" Update:** As Google gets smarter, they're focusing less on keyphrases and more on the meaning, as in topics. The fancy name for this is "semantic search" and Hummingbird is the code name for the new version of Google that does this. So content hubs align perfectly with the direction Google is going. If you've been blogging for a long time, but you're not getting much search traffic, this may be the problem. You're not deliberately creating sets of content, organized around central topics.

- **Social Benefits: Friends with Relevance:** Every social stream is a curated list of posts and conversations. If you direct this stream toward a specific focus, you'll gradually earn followers and attention from people who care about the topic.Now your network will grow in that direction. You'll make friends with people who are relevant to the subject, increasing sharing and building more useful relationships and opportunities to collaborate.

If you're not winning, **you're not done yet.**

- **Mindshare Benefits: Attention and Retention:** When visitors come to learn about a topic, one page may not be enough to satisfy them. But if they find themselves in a hub of content, they'll dig deeper, increases the average pages per visit and average time on site. Give them more and you've got a better chance of being top-of-mind when people think of the topic. Eventually, when people ask "Where was that site that had all that great information on how to do this?" ...they'll think of you and they'll come back.

Example: The "Lead Generation" Topic

Orbit Media builds two kinds of websites: ecommerce sites and lead generation websites. Knowing it would be worth a serious effort to win attention for "lead generation," we decided to target the topic. But the competition for that topic is fierce. So we knew that a page alone would not be enough. We needed a small content hub.

Here's what we created:

- Central hub: "Lead Generation Website Best Practices"
- Infographic: "How to Generate Leads"
- 3 guest blog posts, including "Your Lead Generation Pipeline is Broken" (this post is mistakes and is the evil twin of the best practices content of our hub)

This content was published over several months in several formats on several sites. The central hub was published first on the Orbit site, and subsequent posts all link back to it. We emailed some of these to friends who write and share this kind of content and invited their input.

That was enough. Results kicked in within a few months. Here are the numbers:

- First page one in Google for "lead generation website," alongside some very famous websites.
- A steady stream of 20-40 visits per day from search. These visits would cost $23 per click if we bought them using Adwords. That's about $700 worth of free traffic per day.

- Around 10,000 total visits, including email marketing, social, and referral visits.
- Around 500 social media shares.
- Around 60 newsletter subscribers.
- Links from 12 different sites, including the guest posts and influential friends who mentioned the posts on their sites.

That last number has the added benefit of making our entire domain more credible, making the next mountain / content hub easier to build.

Nothing is hard or easy. But some things take longer than others.

When the attention is valuable, it takes longer to win but it's worth the effort. If you're surrounded by mountains, build tall. Be focused and organized. Build a small mountain of helpful information.

Be the Wikipedia for your industry. Be the People Magazine for the influencers relevant to your audience. Don't make a page, make a section. Don't write a blog post, write a series.

Give the best answers to the questions your audience is asking, and organize those answers into hubs of content. That's how to win online against tough competitors. Let's wrap with a kickass quote from Bruce Lee...

"I fear not the man who has practiced 10,000 kicks once, but I fear the man who has **practiced one kick 10,000 times**."

BRUCE LEE

Promotion

In this chapter, we'll look at specific activities for promoting content. This isn't about the more passive approach of posting search optimized blog posts and then waiting to rank in Google and watching the traffic roll in. This is about taking specific, deliberate action to raise the visibility of your content.

We'll focus on three of the most effective techniques for promoting content:

- Email marketing
- Social media
- Guest blogging

These are the basic activities that professional content marketers use in continuous cycles. Although each could be considered a separate skill, and there are specialized vendors that exclusively focus on one, these techniques are far more effective when used in combination.

If you don't promote your content, you won't get traffic.

Set your expectations for results at the same level as the effort, time and budget you put in.

TIP! As a general rule, you should spend half as much time promoting content as you spend creating it. If you spend two hours writing something, you should spend an hour promoting it.

Email Marketing

In Chapter 2, we looked at the traffic benefits of email marketing. Now let's look in detail at six specific aspects of a successful email marketing campaign.

1. Email Design
When your subscribers open the email, they'll decide within a split second if they want to invest the time to take a look. You need to hook them quickly, and the design of the email is critical. If the email looks like an advertisement with one big flashy graphic, that's generally bad. If the email looks like a page from a book with dense paragraphs and tiny text, that's also bad. You want to give them something in between.

Make a Magazine

A few months ago, I was giving a seminar on email marketing. Before it began, I prepped the room by putting a few things on one of the tables: a book, an advertising insert and a magazine.

As the seminar began I watched people sit at the table and then casually interact with these materials. A few people glanced past the ad then pushed it out of the way. Someone picked up the book and looked at the cover, only to put it down again. But the magazine? The person sitting nearest to it picked it up, sat back in her chair and began flipping through the pages.

Why did the magazine have the most pull? Because it was accessible. The images of the magazine pulled her in and invited her to look, then the words held her attention a bit longer. In less than a second, she was paying attention. Her hand moved, she flipped to a page and she was invested.

The book didn't grab her as fast and looked like a bit more work. The ad may have caught her attention, but she knew what it was and didn't find it very interesting.

Great email marketing does the same thing. It is visual and the content isn't too dense. The content presumably has value and isn't just trying to sell you something. To make your email like a mini-magazine, include the following aspects:

- **Lots of links**
  Research results in Hubspot's Science of Email Marketing show that emails that include more links have a higher clickthrough rate than emails with fewer. Don't be shy about adding links.

REMINDER! Don't forget to add a campaign tracking code using the Google URL Builder described in Chapter 2, so that campaign traffic will appear separately in Analytics. Add the tracking code to all the links to your site from each email.

- **Images**
  See the Images section of Chapter 4.

- **Compelling teasers**
  Include a short excerpt or summary of the article that gets the reader interested. The link to the full article appears after the teaser text. This link may include a call to action such as *Learn the secrets of email marketing* > or may simply say *Read more* >.

Mobile-Friendly Emails

Email messages are very likely to be read on mobile devices. Use the following guidelines to make sure your email design is mobile friendly. See the Mobile section in Chapter 3.

- Left-aligned text.

- Readable and navigable even when images are off. If you use graphical buttons, also add text-based links.

- Small file sizes for quick load time. Avoid large, high-resolution images.

- Test the email by viewing it on various phones. Don't forget to click the links to check the landing pages, which should also be mobile-friendly, if possible.

2. Subject Lines

Competition inside an inbox is fierce and subject lines are critical. They are your hook. If they don't make the recipients curious enough to open your messages, they're not doing their job.

The email subject line is generally the article title, but not always. There is no need to include the target keyphrase since it has nothing to do with SEO. Use whatever will be most compelling to your audience. Be interesting, helpful, emotionally provocative or all three.

See the Inspiration section at the end of this book for a list of writing ideas and headlines, many of which would make excellent subject lines. Also, consider the following tips about specific words and numbers that can impact the results:

Use Words That Improve the Open Rate

The words you choose in your subject line have a direct impact on the percentage of people who open the email. When Hubspot partnered with MailChimp to analyze 9.5 billion emails, they discovered which words are most effective and published the data in a study called "The Science of Email Marketing."

Consider these top-performing words: posts, week's, e-newsletter, digest, bulletin, edition, monthly, latest. They all have something in common: they all indicate that the email is part of a regular series. The recommendation from Dan Zarella, who presented these findings, is to use a subject line that indicates the email is part of a series. *(fig 22a)*

Don't Use Words that Decrease Deliverability

Some words are more likely to be used in spam emails, so spam filters are looking for them. To make sure your emails get through, avoid using these words: *(fig 22b)*

Consider the worst-performing words: raffle, rewards, 10%, coupon, 15%, discount, savings, offer. They all have something in common: they're frequently used in advertising. Emails with these words in the subject line are probably trying to sell you something, rather than inform or help you.

If you're even tempted to use these words in your subject lines, you haven't embraced the central principle of content marketing: to help your business by first helping others through useful content, not advertising.

Odd Numbers

Next time you find yourself in a store checkout aisle, notice the magazine headlines. See any numbers? Magazine publishers and content marketers seem to have a fondness for odd numbers. Perhaps odd numbers are perceived as more credible or scientific.

I'll admit, it's difficult to resist the temptation and I've used this technique many times. I suspect an email called "3 ways to get more 7-step articles in your top 10 lists" would have a nice clickthrough rate.

Odd or even, numerals stand out in lines of text. Using numeric characters can make an email subject line (and its blog post headline) more prominent in the recipient's inbox or Twitter stream.

Most Clicked
Subject Line Words

Fig. 22a

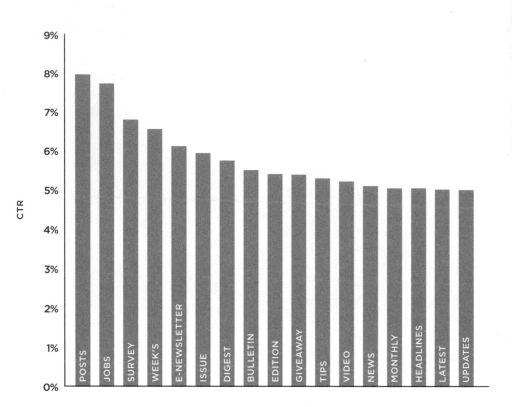

Most Abused
Subject Line Words

Fig. 22b

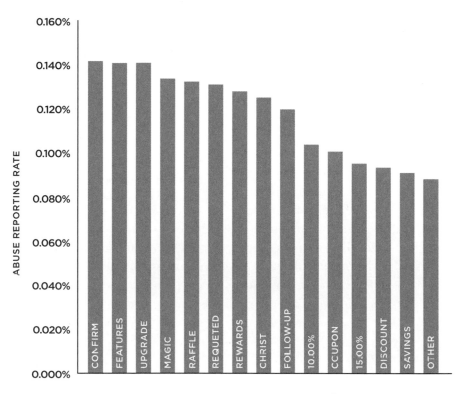

3. Sender Name

The "sender name" is a huge factor in building trust and increasing open rates. Many marketers forget to check this, but no email recipients forget to look. Along with the subject line, it's all you've got. Use it to build enough trust to earn the click.

If the sender name includes a person's name in addition to the brand, the email is more likely to be opened. For example, an email from "Susan Clark | Zippy Accountants" will have a higher open rate than an email from "Zippy Accountants."

The sender name isn't the same as the "from" address. Don't use "sclark@zippycpa.com" as your sender name. And "Do Not Reply" isn't a friendly name to call yourself.

The sender name is easy to change from within your email service provider. Some even make it easy to test different sender names with an A/B test. Half of your list gets the email with one sender name, the other half receive it with a different sender name. Now you can see how various sender names can affect the open rate.

4. List Growth

The size and quality of your list outstrips all other factors in the success of email marketing efforts. Here are a few basic principles for growing a large and engaged readership. The key is to get permission but be aggressive.

Sales Activity = Subscriber Opportunities

If the salesperson was friendly and helpful, and the content is good, the new subscribers will be likely to open and read your emails. Actual prospects are your most valuable subscribers!

Is it ok to add people to your list without asking for their permission?

Yes, but your standards should be very high. Seth Godin once wrote a blog post suggesting that you add anyone to the list who would complain if you didn't add them. For example, our job at Orbit Media is to help our clients with their web marketing. They would be unhappy if we didn't share our latest web marketing techniques with them, so we add our clients to the list.

WARNING! It is illegal and inconsiderate to send unsolicited commercial email if the recipients have no way to unsubscribe. Although "spam" is any unsolicited email and generally a terrible idea, it is only illegal if recipients cannot remove themselves from the list. Make sure that every marketing email you send includes a link that allows the recipient to unsubscribe. These links are typically added automatically by the email service provider.

Properties of a Good Email Signup Form

To succeed in email marketing, you need to build a great list. To build a great list, your site needs a good email signup form. This section is about email signup forms and how they affect email subscriptions. This is very important to anyone doing email marketing.

There are four main factors in visitor subscriptions. Coincidentally, they all start with 'P'.

- **Prominence**: The signup form is highly visible on the page; it's large, uses contrasting colors and appears in several places.

- **Promise**: There is a description of the benefits to subscribing, what kind of information to expect, how frequently. In other words, "What's in it for me?" (WIIFM)

- **Proof**: There's evidence that it's legitimate, especially social proof, such as a testimonial or number of subscribers.

Fig. 23a

> **Join the World's Largest Marketing Community**
>
> **IT'S FREE!** Become a member to get the tools and knowledge you need to market smarter.
>
> your email here!
>
> **SIGN UP**
>
> we respect your privacy.
>
> **Stay connected ... follow us!**

Fig. 23b

The Orbiter

We like to share our thoughts about web strategy, usability, SEO, marketing, design inspiration, web video, & really anything that strikes our fancy. **Want to subscribe?**

Fig. 23c

The Orbiter

"Your posts are always so carefully written and with such impactful messages, I love reading them. Thank you for the killer posts..." - Kevin K.

> Join over 7,500 people who receive bi-weekly web marketing tips.
>
> Email Address
>
> SIGN-UP!

- **Privacy**: Assure the subscriber that they won't receive spam and that you won't share their information with anyone else.

Here are five examples of email signup forms, good and bad.

Example: Marketing Profs

This form is doing everything right to maximize subscriptions. It's got all four p's.

It's *prominent* on the page. It's both large and a separate color.

The *promise* made is the content "tools and knowledge you need to market smarter."

The *proof* is in the header: "World's Largest Marketing Community." Sounds good!

Even *privacy* is addressed with a small link.

(fig 23a)

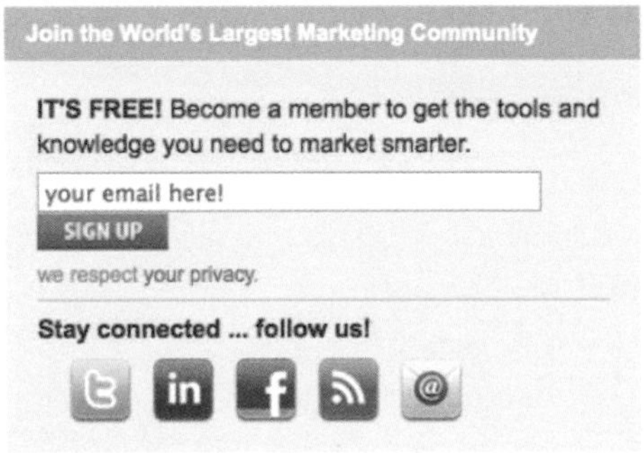

Example: Orbit Media

At Orbit, for years we had a link at the top of the blog that let visitors click to get to a page with a signup box. It looked like this: *(fig. 23b)*

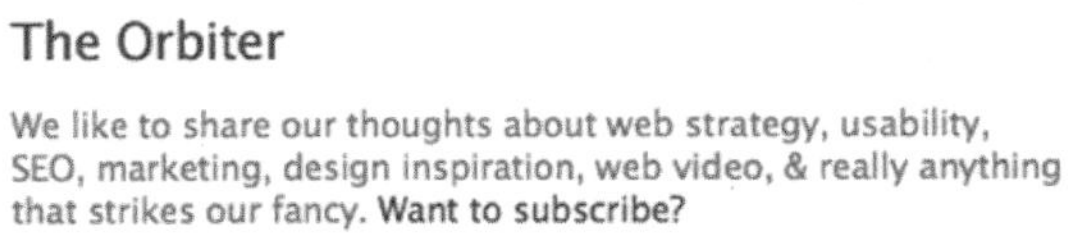

Then one day, we made a change. We let people subscribe without leaving the page. So now the signup form looks like this: *(fig. 23c)*

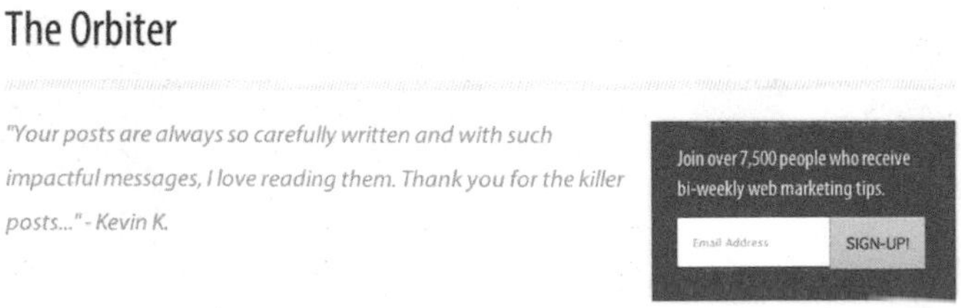

And here's what happened. Look at the Google Analytics for weekly signups and conversion rates, this year and last year... *(fig. 23d)*

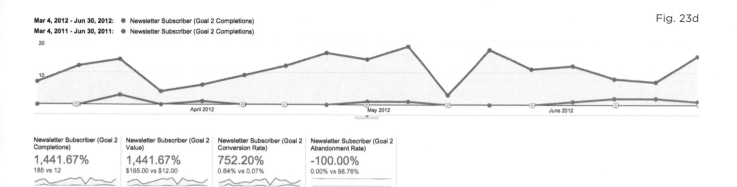

Fig. 23d

Yes, you are reading that right. **That's a 750% increase in the conversion rate leading to a 1400% increase in subscriptions.** Aside from the change to the form, the only change we've made in our marketing is an increase in the frequency of publishing in May and June.

TIP! Once visitors subscribe, they'll arrive at a thank-you page and get a confirmation email. Take advantage of these additional touch points by gently inviting them to connect with you through other channels such as Facebook, Twitter, LinkedIn and Google+.

TIP! When you get new subscribers, you might want to email them to welcome them to the list. This email will thank them for signing up, give them an idea of what to expect and remind them to keep an eye out for the newsletter. Remind them to add you to their "whitelist" to keep you out of their spam folder. These welcome emails can be sent automatically by setting up an auto-responder. Contact your web designer or email service provider for details.

New subscribers from your site is an important metric to track in Analytics and should be set up as a separate goal. This will allow you to test and improve the sign-up form's prominence and call to action.

Stay Connected

For many B2B companies, a relatively small number of high-value connections is better than a large number of low-value connections. If you sell insurance or if you're an attorney, a lead is potentially very valuable and quality is more important than quantity. If you're a B2C company selling T-shirts or chocolate, an individual transaction isn't worth quite as much, so quantity is likely more important than quality.

If you're in a B2B business, it's worth taking the time to keep an eye on which emails don't get through. Watch your "bounces." Emails often bounce when people move from one company to another. Every bounced email is an opportunity to keep in touch with people and connect with new businesses.

Find people on LinkedIn to see where they went, then connect with them and ask if they would like to stay subscribed. If so, you can get their new email addresses and re-subscribe them. If the connection with these people was real and they valued your content, they'll happily agree to stay on your list.

TIP! It's easier to maintain connections when you combine social media with email marketing. You may lose touch via email, but LinkedIn, Twitter, Facebook and Google+ connections remain in place.

5. When to Send…and How Often

Timing is everything. Let's look at Hubspot's research on the impact of timing and frequency of email marketing.

Timing

The day of the week makes a difference. Although most businesses wouldn't think of it, the research suggests that sending marketing emails on a weekend is a good thing. Saturdays and Sundays have higher clickthrough rates. *(fig. 24a)*

Impact on unsubscriptions supports the case for weekend emails. Subscribers are slightly more likely to unsubscribe earlier in the week. *(fig. 24b)*

The time of day is another way to fine-tune your email marketing. The research suggests that early morning is a better time to send email. *(fig. 24c)*

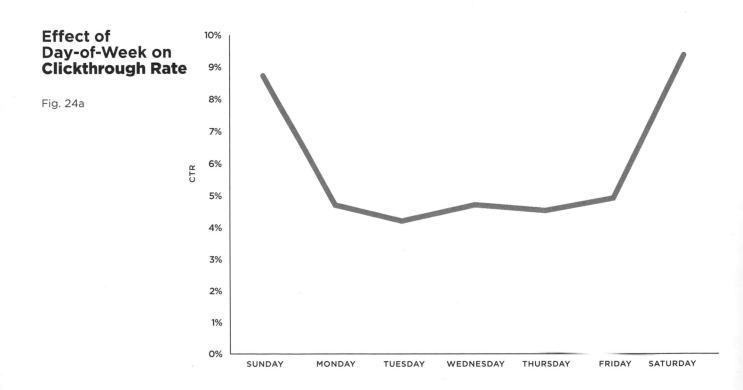

Effect of Day-of-Week on Clickthrough Rate

Fig. 24a

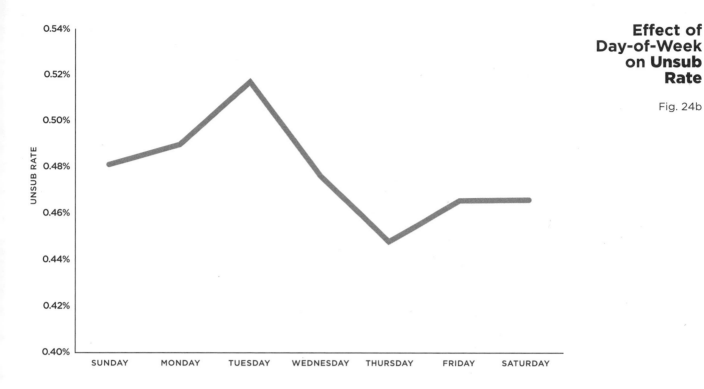

Effect of Day-of-Week on Unsub Rate

Fig. 24b

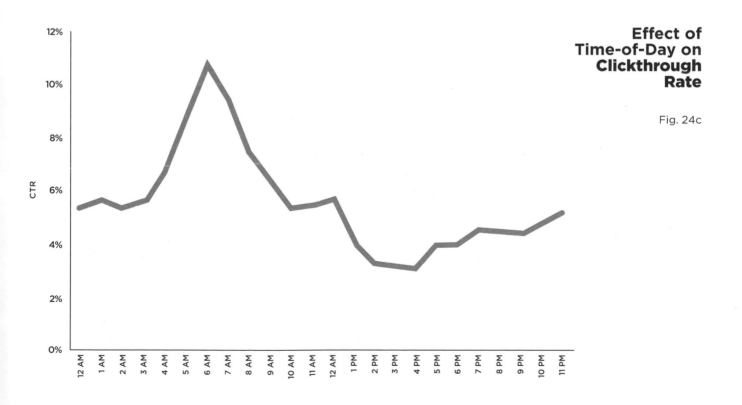

Effect of Time-of-Day on Clickthrough Rate

Fig. 24c

It's likely that your subscribers have set aside some time to read email in the morning, which can lead to dramatically higher clickthrough rates. In the late afternoon, most of us are in "clean-up" mode and trying to process many things quickly before shutting down for the day.

Every list is different and success will depend on the preferences of your target audience. As always, it's important to experiment with timing. Try doing exactly what the research suggests, or assume that this is what everyone else is doing and try counter-competitive timing.

Once you find something that seems to work, stick with it for a while. This will help set the expectation that your email is coming. They might not rush to their inbox every Wednesday at 9:30 AM ready to click, but they won't be surprised to see your message then, either.

If the quality of the content is very high, the timing is less important. People will hold on to it and read it when they're ready. They may read it many times. If you check your email stats days or weeks later, and the clickthrough rates are still trickling upward, you will know you wrote something good.

Frequency

No one can open or click your emails if you don't send them. So far, we've looked at the factors that can increase the rate that people open and click emails, but the total amount of traffic you drive also depends on how frequently you send. This is a huge factor!

So how often should you send email newsletters? The answer: *as often as you can consistently produce relevant, useful content.*

- **Minimum frequency**
  You should send often enough that you stay in people's minds. But also consider the length of the sales cycle of your product or service. If it takes one month for a prospect to meet a competitor and buy from them instead, your email frequency should be every two weeks at a minimum.

- **Maximum frequency**
  Yes, there is a point at which you may actually annoy people by sending too frequently, but if your content is good, you might be surprised at how often you can send successful email campaigns. I've heard many people say, "My subscribers don't want to get email that often," but when I dig deeper, I find they've never tested the limit, or they got one or two negative comments and backed off completely.

Yes, if you send more frequently, the percentage of people who click on every email may drop, but your goal is traffic, not a high clickthrough rate. Consider this: Even if your clickthrough rates drop by half, sending email weekly rather than monthly will double your traffic. You'll get half the traffic from each email, but you're sending four times as often.

6. Measure and Improve

As with everything in content marketing, the key to successful email marketing is to experiment, measure, iterate and improve. Many email service providers make A/B testing easy by allowing you to try different times of day, days of the week, and designs and subject lines, all using the same list and isolating the other variables.

Watch the Analytics carefully and listen for feedback. If you think there is an opportunity to improve, don't be afraid to redesign your template, send at a different time or tweak your frequency. If it doesn't work out, you can try something else in the next email.

Final note on email: perhaps more than any other channel, *successful email marketing depends on the quality of the content*. To convince your subscribers that your next newsletter is worth opening and clicking, you must make *this* newsletter interesting and useful. Build trust through consistent quality in your email content, or watch your email stats degrade over time.

Create your publishing calendar, set the due dates for writing and editing, keep an eye toward list growth, and then send, test, measure and send again.

Social Promotion

It's true. Thanks to social media, there is no need to hope and wait for visitors to find you by searching, and no need to put all your eggs in one email marketing basket. With social media, there are actions you can take right now that will drive a bit of traffic within the hour.

NOTE! The effectiveness of the recommendations within this section depends on how well you've built your personal networks within the social networks. If you have no presence on Twitter, Facebook, Google+ or LinkedIn, social promotion won't work. Build up an engaged, relevant audience with consistent, positive interaction. Talk to people. Help people. Promote their content, then let them help you promote yours.

Post on the Networks: Facebook, Twitter, LinkedIn, etc.

The first step in social media promotion is posting on the networks. Generally speaking, all content should be posted on all networks. It's possible that some fans and followers will see the same post more than once, but don't worry about overwhelming them. It may prompt them to take a closer look and give them more options to share.

CAUTION! Blog posts without pictures will not be as prominent or pretty when posted on Facebook, Twitter and LinkedIn. Make sure that each post has at least one image.

- Facebook
- Google+
- LinkedIn
- Secondary networks
  StumbleUpon, Delicious, Pinterest, Reddit, Digg, etc.

  Other web communities: local associations, networking groups, industry directories or any site where you have an account, can log in and post content.

When posting to a network, you are basically adding a link and a teaser. The teaser is a headline and a short excerpt from the full post. There is no risk of a duplicate content penalty in Google, but you still don't want to put the entire post in the teaser. If the teaser is too long, the reader may glean all the meaning and value without clicking and becoming a visitor.

You'll also have an opportunity to mention others when posting on Facebook, Google+ and Twitter. Take this opportunity to share the post with one or two fans or friends who are likely to read, enjoy and comment on the post.

Google+ allows you to add formatting to your headline and teaser: bolding, italics and bullets. Take advantage of this formatting to draw attention to your teaser by bolding the headline and using bullets to summarize the main points.

Formatting	Shortcut
Bolding	Add an asterisk (*) to both sides of the text EXAMPLE: This text is *bold* This text is **bold**
Italics	Add an underscore (_) to both sides of the text EXAMPLE: This text is _italicized_ This text is *italicized*
Strikethrough	Add a hyphen to both sides of the text EXAMPLE: This text is -struck through- This text is ~~struck through~~
Bullets	Alt + 8 adds a bullet point. EXAMPLE: • Point one • Point two

If you are active within Facebook groups, LinkedIn groups or any other forums, you have another opportunity to promote your content. As long as the content is relevant to the topics within that group, feel free to share it there. If the post sparks comments or conversation, be prepared to respond. It's not polite to join a group and post content without engaging with people.

If you have both a personal following and a business with its own following, consider first posting the content on the business page, then sharing from your personal account (example: post on Orbit's Facebook page, then share the post from Andy's account). This will leverage your personal connections while guiding others toward the brand.

TIP! After you post a nice piece of high-value original content, the timing is right to take deliberate steps to grow your social following. Just as the content on a web page determines the visitors' likelihood to convert, your most recent post on Twitter or Google+ will appear at the top of your stream and will determine the likelihood of a new potential fan to follow you or add you to a circle. They may be less likely to follow or circle you if your top post is irrelevant to their interests or about cats.

Once the post is live on Twitter and Google+, take a moment to search those networks for people who are likely to be interested in the topic of your post. If you wrote about technology solutions for executives, search for "CTO." If your article is about a new farmers market in Atlanta, search for gardeners in the area. Follow these people or add them to a circle; they may notice you, see the post, follow you back and possibly share it.

Tweet!

The next step is send out a series of Tweets. One Tweet isn't likely to be effective, so we recommend a series of Tweets spread out over time. Depending on your level of activity on Twitter, it may be appropriate to Tweet an article 4-6 times over two weeks or ten times over a month.

⚠️ **WARNING!** Your Twitter stream should not be dominated by Tweets promoting your content. No more than 20% of your Tweets should include links to your content. The remaining 80% should be conversations with your followers, promoting others' content, witty observations, inspirational quotes, thank-you messages, etc.

These Tweets should include various ways of summarizing the article. They should not all be the same. Although one of them may simply be the article headline and the link, others should include variations of the headline and/or other elements:

- **Mentions** of people at the end of the Tweet (see targeted sharing below)

Andy Crestodina @crestodina   1m
Nice Blogs Finish Last convinceandconvert.com/blogging-and-c...
cc: @manamica

- **Hashtags** of keyphrases or topics (but no need to overdo it)

Andy Crestodina @crestodina   1m
Nice Blogs Finish Last convinceandconvert.com/blogging-and-c...
#blogging

- **Quotes** from the article

Andy Crestodina @crestodina   1m
Nice Blogs Finish Last convinceandconvert.com/blogging-and-c...
"Only 34% of businesses align content with the buying stages"

Although a Tweet can include up to 140 characters (which should be plenty of room for your Tweets) try to keep the length down to 120 characters to make retweeting easier and more likely. Why? When people retweet something, they may want to add a little something to it. If you leave them some room, they are more likely to mention you.

💡 **TIP!** For a great overview on the mechanics of Twitter, see Jessica Hische's beautiful explanation, *Mom This is How Twitter Works*.

> When people retweet something, they may want to add a little something to it. If you **leave them some room**, they are more likely to mention you.

It's not necessary (or possible) to summarize the entire article within these Tweets. The Tweet is simply intended to be a hook to entice the reader to click. For example, when Tweeting an article on five ways businesses can use Pinterest, consider sending a short Tweet that indicates the meaning of the article without giving too much away, such as "This is why I love Pinterest." This leaves a little mystery. It pulls the reader in. Although I may not be in the mood to read a top 5 list about Pinterest, I might want to find out what you love about it.

> *"Twitter is the greatest content distribution network out there for people who create content. Everyone gets that. Twitter didn't start out with that idea, but that's what it became because they kind of stepped back and let us use it the way we want to. What choice really, do they have?" - Brian Clark, Copyblogger (Internet Marketing for Smart People)*

It's not necessary (or possible) to summarize the entire article within these Tweets. The Tweet is simply intended to be **a hook to entice the reader** to click.

TIP! Although URL shorteners condense the link and allow for tracking, they also hide the domain name, and thus, remove information from the Tweet. Now that URLs in Tweets sent from Twitter.com are shortened automatically, you may find that URL shorteners are unnecessary or even less effective.

Example: Which of the following links is more compelling to the dentist that reads it?

• bit.ly/38Ud8s

• dentistrytips.com/blog...

TIP! Consider promoting your content through social channels one day before promoting it through email marketing. Readers from social sources are more likely to comment, and a post with a few comments will look better when the surge of email visitors arrive. If you moderate your comments before making them live, be prepared to approve comments quickly. If these comments include feedback for ways to make the content stronger, don't hesitate to do some quick editing before sending the mass email.

ADVANCED TIP! If you track the clickthrough rates from Tweets using a URL shortener, you can see which Tweets generate the most clicks to an individual article, then use that Tweet as a subject line in your email marketing. Using Twitter to A/B test email subject lines is a fun but imperfect science, and only possible for companies with large followings.

Who are you looking for? Whether it's new talent, customers, or just friends, we help find whom you're after.
Login with Twitter and we'll overlay your follow status. Want precise tracking of new/lost followers?

| Q SEO Poet | | search Twitter profiles | ▾ | Do It | Examples: CEOs, SEO, social media, most followers, oldest, & most influence |

more options

Showing 1 - 50 of 66 results (order by relevance)

No filters ▾				tweets ⬍	following ⬍	followers ▾	days old ⬍	Social Authority ⬍
follow ⊘ ⊘		**Steve Akins** @SteveAkinsSEO Digital Marketing Strategist, **SEO**, Developer, Entrepreneur, Struggling **Poet** :), Gastronome, Explorer	Chicago	44,648	14,857	14,546	2,012	47
follow ⊘ ⊘		**Jaime Lynn Smith** @ThoughtsFurPaws Passionate pet blogger, animal welfare advocate/volunteer; Pet360 blogger, WAPN contributor, TeddyHilton writer, **SEO** Copywriter, published **poet**, love outdoors	Cleveland, Ohio	13,635	4,039	7,359	1,952	36
follow ⊘ ⊘		**Ilin Ivan** @IvanCoFox http://t.co/vAx8BHYjDw - subscribe ! **Poet**, sci-fi writer, sport publicist, delphi developer, profi kapper #BitCoin #BTC #EarnMoney #**SEO** #BetTips #Kapper	Saint-Petersburg, Pskov, Minsk	12,545	5,287	4,835	762	36

Targeted Sharing

If you take a few minutes to find the people who are likely to be interested in your content, you'll get better results when you share. Part of the beauty of Twitter is that you can find almost anyone imaginable. So it's not difficult to find someone who's likely to care about your content.

Twitter itself has a notoriously bad search tool, but there are many other tools that make up for this. Here's an example of how I used one of those tools to find people and promote a blog post.

The post in this case is called "Web Marketing Poetry: SEO Advice in Rhyming Quatrains." It's a poem that compares the constraints of writing for search marketing to the constraints of rhyming in poetry. People interested in both SEO and poetry would love this one, right?

Currently, the Twitter Advanced Search (https://twitter.com/search-advanced) doesn't allow you to search users' bios, so use a tool like Followerwonk (http://followerwonk.com). Select "Search Twitter bios."

I entered "SEO poet" and clicked search. *(fig. 25a)*

It turned out that, of the 140,000,000,000 people on Twitter, there are 31 who have "SEO" and "poet" in their bios. Scrolling through and reading the bios, I saw that they were indeed people who are both poets and search optimizers, the perfect audience for my post.

Next I wrote a simple Tweet and mentioned a few of these people at the end.

NOTE! I would typically link directly to the article, but in this case, I hoped this article got traction within another network, StumbleUpon. So I used the link to the article within that network. This gave people the opportunity to "like" it on StumbleUpon, possibly leading to more traffic down the road.

Fig. 25b

Andy Crestodina @crestodina   13h
It's a poem about writing for SEO.
stumbleupon.com/su/1B9pMi/www.... cc: @SukhSandhu @egabbert
@steveakinsseo.

SukhSandhu   5 pts
Its beautiful, It was fun reading this. Thanks for sharing :)
12 HOURS AGO   Like Reply

Sukh Sandhu @SukhSandhu **retweeted to 27,238 followers:**

crestodina Andy Crestodina
It's a poem about writing for SEO. stumbleupon.com/su/1B9pMi/www.... cc:
@SukhSandhu @egabbert @steveakinsseo.
Mar 31, 10:33 PM via web

Andy Crestodina @crestodina   13h
It's a poem about writing for SEO.
stumbleupon.com/su/1B9pMi/www.... cc: @SukhSandhu @egabbert
@steveakinsseo.
↳ Retweeted by Sukh Sandhu

Sukh Sandhu @SukhSandhu   12h
I just left a comment in "Web Marketing Poetry" fyre.it/SPh

In less than an hour, Sukh Sandhu, the first person mentioned in the Tweet, visited the post and left a comment.

He also Retweeted it to his 27,000 followers and then Tweeted that he had commented. *(fig. 25b)*

There is absolutely nothing spammy about sharing your content with people whom you feel would enjoy it. In this case, I was confident that they would like the post and I simply invited them to read it, knowing we have similar interests (poetry and search marketing). In this case, Sukh literally thanked me for sharing it in his comment. Naturally, I thanked him for back for the comment and for sharing it on Twitter.

TIP! Some commenting tools make this kind of sharing more likely. LiveFyre and Disqus are WordPress commenting systems that make the comments section more of a conversation. They let commenters login using Twitter or Facebook, which is both easier and pulls in their profile pictures. The tools also make it very simple for commenters to announce on Twitter or Facebook that they left a comment.

I have very low expectations when I do this targeted sharing, but it always seems to work. Usually, if I mention two or three people, one of them responds. And the entire exercise takes less than five minutes.

It's not surprising that targeted sharing is effective, because it is so precise. If you're a Star Trek fan who helps nonprofits with fundraising and one day you see a Tweet that days "Mr. Spock's Guide to Silent Auctions," wouldn't you click on it? You'd be thrilled to read it! And grateful to whomever shared with you.

Email: Manual, Old School, Social Sharing

It's not fancy, but it's effective. Email your content directly to specific contacts. They don't need to be subscribed to your email list. You're just sharing something relevant along with a personal note with a high-value contact, who could be a prospect, a journalist, a job candidate or an industry thought-leader.

This is especially important for businesses where the value of a transaction is very high. If you sell helicopters or provide wealth management services, and you've created a relevant, informative article about the latest in in-flight controls or tax law changes, send the article to recent prospects individually via email. They are already in your funnel. Arguably, there are no readers more important than these.

TIP! If the potential reader is extremely valuable, you can use a URL shortener when creating the link for the email. If you use this shortened link nowhere else, you'll be able to see if the recipient clicked the link.

Example: If I wanted Seth Godin to review this book and I send him a link to a downloadable file, I might shorten the link through bit.ly before sending it to Mr. Godin. Since I would have used this link only in this way, I can check back on bit.ly to see the traffic. One click means Seth downloaded the book. Zero clicks means he didn't.

ECHO...Echo...echo

If you've done a good job promoting the content through social channels, it has likely been shared in the networks and retweeted within Twitter. Now you have an opportunity to increase the visibility by creating a mini-echo chamber of conversation. Here's how:

- If the content was shared by others on Facebook and Google+, comment on the new shares with a thank-you. If there's a conversation happening within the comments, jump in.

It's not fancy, **but it's effective**. Email your content directly to specific contacts.

- If the content was retweeted, thank the person who shared it. The thank-yous and responses can easily triple the number of Tweets related to a piece of content.

- If the article generated comments, respond to them. Then find the commenters on the social networks and let them know you've responded.

- If the article generated lots of traffic, shares, comments, etc., Tweet about the popularity of the article: "Wow! Everyone seems to like this post..."

The idea is to create a small feedback loop and take advantage of any activity by responding. This can extend what is often a very short life of content within social networks. It increases the chance of content being noticed and becoming more viral.

Timing is important since within Facebook and Google+, posts that have lots of activity (likes, +1s and clicks) stay at the top of people's streams for longer. Be ready to have conversations, say thank you and respond to comments when social promotion begins.

Consider Tweeting links to articles published months or even years ago. These "from the archive" or "encore" Tweets can revive posts buried deep within your blog. If your audience has grown since they were first posted, it's likely that many of your followers haven't seen these yet. As long as the article doesn't contain out-of-date information, it may still be relevant and useful.

Guest Blogging

I consider guest blogging to be a content promotion tactic because it leverages the audience and influence of others to improve the visibility of content and companies.

There are two sides to guest blogging: publishing your content on other sites (being a guest blogger) and seeking content from others for your site (blogger relations and guest blogger outreach). They are both powerful content marketing tactics with search marketing and social media benefits.

To understand the benefits of guest blogging, especially when combined, let's imagine the processes and outcomes of two bloggers: one blogger who posts only on his own site, and another who embraces both approaches to guest blogging.

Round One: Both Bloggers Create Two Posts

Blogger A has written two posts and publishes both on his blog. *(fig. 26a)*

Blogger B has also written two posts, but rather than post them both on her blog, she connects with another website owner or content manager who agrees to publish one of her posts. She asks only for a link back to her site in exchange. This link is indicated by the dotted line in the diagram above.

Also, she reaches out to another writer in her field. This writer submits a new, original post and Blogger B publishes it on her site. This guest post is indicated by the red box above.

Let's see how they're doing:

Scoreboard	Posts	Links	Social Connections
Blogger A	2	0	0
Blogger B	3	1	2

Although Blogger B only wrote two of the posts, she now has three posts associated with her brand. She also has a link and a few new friends.

> Consider Tweeting links to articles **published months or even years ago**. These "from the archive" or "encore" Tweets can revive posts buried deep within your blog.

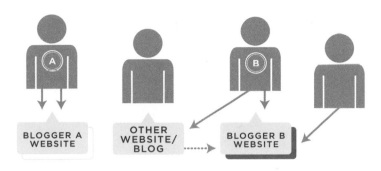

Round Two:
Both Bloggers Have Published Four Posts

Blogger A has now written and published four posts, all on his own blog. *(fig. 26b)*

Blogger B has published two posts on external websites, both of which now have links back to her site. She's also connected with expert writers who have contributed two relevant posts that are now on her blog. And she's built connections with the people behind other websites relevant to her business.

Scoreboard	Posts	Links	Social Connections
Blogger A	4	0	0
Blogger B	6	2	4

Round Three:
Both Bloggers Have Created Eight Posts

Blogger A has consistently produced and published content, but...

Blogger B has created a network of content, both on her site and linked to her brand. This has increased exposure to her content. She's also growing a network of connections with experts, which has increased her influence in her field. This is what great web marketing looks like. *(fig. 26c)*

Scoreboard	Posts	Links	Social Connections
Blogger A	8	0	0
Blogger B	12	4	8

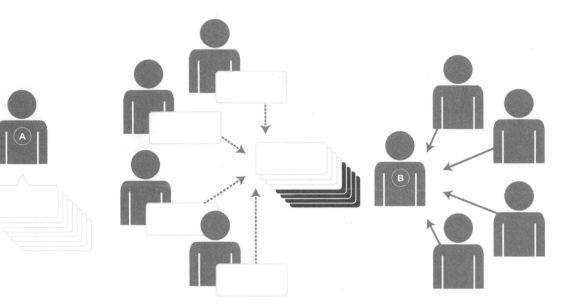

Fig. 26c

Remember, search engine optimization is about great content and great links. Social media is about real connections with real people. Guest blogging provides both.

Target Host Blogs

Different blogs will have different benefits to your content marketing so it's important to understand the options and outcomes. There are generally two types of guest blogging opportunities: local social blogs or national topical blogs.

	Local	National
Primary benefit	Sociál media	Search engine optimization
Criteria	Large social following and readership	Authoritative domain, linking opportunity

Local and Social Blogs
Good for branding and networking (social media).

These could be high-traffic local sites such as local media sites. They may cover a broad range of topics, but they are generally focused on your region. The ideal local blogs are those with large social media followings and lots of comments on previous blog posts. The readers of these blogs may be relevant people in your area that you'd like to meet in person someday.

TIP! When possible, it's good to guest blog more than once on sites like these, so the readers see you repeatedly and become more likely to remember you.

National and Topical Blogs

Good for link building (SEO).

Although any guest blogging opportunity has some social benefit, sometimes guest blogging is more focused on the benefit of the possible link back to your site. For this reason, the size of the blog's readership or social following is less important and the authority of the domain is more important (more on measuring domain authority soon).

These sites may be tightly focused on your industry, such as trade publications or association websites. These may be websites of businesses like yours in other parts of the country. Regardless, the topics of the posts on these blogs are related to the topics that are important to your audience. The fact that these sites are topically related to your product or service means they offer a stronger SEO benefit. A link from a site that is relevant to your business is better than a link from a random or irrelevant site.

Example: If your business repairs HVAC systems for hospitals, look for links from mechanical contractor associations, repair safety sites or even healthcare blogs.

TIP! It's less important to blog repeatedly on these websites, since the value of the subsequent links is not likely to be as strong as a new link from a second, separate host blog. When your focus is SEO, one of your main goals is to increase the total number of websites that link to you. So you'd rather have two links from two different sites than two links from the same site.

If you're able to find a site that meets both criteria—social and search—patiently cultivate a close relationship and seek to position yourself as a regular contributor or columnist.

How to Measure the Value of a Guest Blogging Opportunity...and a Link

In Chapter 1 we explored the research on why websites rank in search engines and we learned the importance of incoming links. We know that the quality of these links, not just the number of them, plays a huge part in search rankings. Not all links are created equal. If we're going to be effective in our efforts to improve our "link profile," we must learn to estimate the value of a possible link.

Here is an oversimplification that will help explain this concept: In the eyes of Google, the Internet is a network of authority and trust. Some sites are more trustworthy than others, largely because other trustworthy sites link to them. Sites that have few or no incoming links are not as trusted, because other sites have not passed along their trust through links.

> Links are votes of trust. All things being equal (of course, they never are), a site with more, higher-quality links will outrank a site with fewer, lower-quality links.

Search engine optimizers call this trust "link juice." Some sites have a lot and others have very little. Ideally, trusted websites link to you and that juice flows through your site via internal links. A link from a trusted site may pass 1,000 times more trust than an unknown, untrusted site.

Link Metrics and Analysis

Open Site Explorer was created by Moz and is an invaluable industry-standard tool for measuring link popularity and authority. In addition to showing the approximate raw number of incoming links, it shows several other metrics including domain authority, page authority, MozRank and MozTrust. The original metric for measuring trust and authority is Google's own PageRank (named after Google founder Larry Page), which is a simpler one-to-ten estimate of link popularity.

Unless you are a full-time search optimizer or really obsessed with link building, I encourage you to focus on domain authority when estimating a general value of a link or guest blogging opportunity. You certainly could consider other metrics when evaluating a possible website for guest blogging (some people pay attention only to PageRank or Alexa Traffic Rank), but for most web marketers, Domain Authority is sufficient. It's a good, general rating of the trustworthiness of a website.

How to Use Open Site Explorer

WARNING! If you are not a paid subscriber to Moz Pro, you will be able to use this tool only a few times each day from any given computer. I consider Moz to be an indispensable tool for content marketing, and recommend spending the $100 per month for the Pro subscription. It includes many useful tools. One tool tracks search rankings over time. Another tool makes prioritized recommendations for keyphrase usage on specific pages.

This tool is as easy to use as Google itself. Just visit the site and enter the address of the possible host blog. It will show you the number of incoming links, the number of domains with incoming links, the page authority and the domain authority. The higher the better.

If the domain authority is below 40, a link to your site from this site would have low value, unless the domain authority of your site is even lower. If it's in the 40-70 range, it's worth pursuing. If it's in the 70s or 80s, it's worth pursuing patiently and persistently. Links from sites in the 90-100 range are generally unattainable through guest blogging, but may be possible though "newsjacking" or other clever, well-timed PR techniques.

CAUTION! Some blogs may add a tiny piece of code to their links that drastically reduce (if not completely eliminate) the value of a link. The code is robots="nofollow" and they add it to keep the value of their links to themselves and also to be less attractive to link spammers.

Although you may still want to guest blog for the social and branding benefits on sites that use this code, keep in mind that guest posts here will have little or no SEO benefit. Look at the HTML of other posts and examine the links to see if this code is there.

Therefore, the ideal link to your site and the ideal sites to target for guest blogging are:

- Sites that have high domain authority
- Sites that allow you to use target keyphrases in the link to your site (remember the importance of keyphrases in anchor text from Chapter 2)
- Sites that don't use the robots="nofollow" code within your link

⚠ **CAUTION!** Guest blogging has become an abused (or at least, overused) tactic as some search optimizers have started to send spam email to blogs offering piles of "unique" content, ready to be posted. Google has finally said they are taking action to reduce the SEO value of this tactic. So think of the big picture, the branding value and the readers. If you focus on guest blogging as a form of PR with some possible SEO value, you'll still find huge benefits with this approach.

How to Submit Your Content

Once you've got a few host blogs in your sights, it's time to reach out and see if they are interested in your content. Keep in mind that the owners of popular sites with powerful domains are contacted regularly by eager content marketers. You need to be thoughtful and considerate when making contact with them, just as PR professionals are thoughtful and considerate when contacting journalists.

They might have a "guest blog for us" page with a contact form. If there are guest blogging guidelines posted, read them carefully. In other cases, you submit your request through a general contact form or to a general email address on a contact page. I've even seen hopeful guest bloggers approach website owners openly within comments on Google+ and on Twitter. It's a bold approach, but it's not usually effective.

Here are some DOs and DON'Ts to follow when submitting a possible guest post:

- **Don't waste their time**
  A little research and consideration go a long way. Make sure that you're submitting content that would make sense on the site and be interesting to its readers. I once absent-mindedly submitted a gritty Bruce Willis–themed web marketing article to a very pink, feminine web design blog. That didn't go well.

Keep in mind that the owners of popular sites with powerful domains are **contacted regularly** by eager content marketers.

- **Do convey the value of the content**
Take a moment to explain how the content fits within their blog and would be useful to their audience. You had better sincerely believe in the value of the content! Be confident but brief. A few sentences will do.

    If you optimized the content by aligning it with a keyphrase, mention that here. You can even mention the popularity of the phrase.

- **Don't be pushy**
Remember they are the host and you are the aspiring guest. You're inviting yourself over to their home (or at least homepage). You should be very polite. Offer to let them make any edits, change the headline or images, even remove any links if they feel they are inappropriate. Be friendly.

- **Do offer to help promote it**
If you have a significant social following, let them know you'll be promoting the article through your social networks. Of course you would do this anyway, but drawing attention to your ability to drive traffic will make your content more attractive.

    If the post is likely to get comments, offer to be available once it goes live to add responses and answer questions within the comments.

- **Do follow up**
Thank the host blog with an email. If the article ranks, let them know and they'll appreciate it. If you feel the post was successful, consider offering to write another. Now is the best time to grow the relationship with your new friends and collaborators.

TIP! If possible, submit the final, edited version of the content to the host blog in HTML format. It may take a bit of skill (or HTML authoring software like Dreamweaver), but it will make it easier for them to post and help assure that the links, formatting and images are kept in place. At the very least, submit the author box information as HTML, since it includes the all-important link to your site and the links to your social media profiles.

Don't be discouraged if you have trouble placing a post. You may submit an article to five or more blogs before it gets accepted. If you have trouble getting something published, consider these options:

- Write posts that are specifically tailored for the target blog. First, research which headlines and posts are the most successful on their site (i.e., which ones get lots of comments).

- Submit ideas for posts to target blogs that relate to something they just posted within the last day. If they like the idea, you have a toe in the door.

- Network on social media with the editors before submitting.

- Submit posts to many potential blogs at once. Let each know that it's original content but you're submitting it to several other sites. First come first served!

- Submit posts to lower-value sites.

- Rewrite the headline of the post or scrap it completely.

TIP! Carry a printed writing sample of one of your best articles with you. If you meet another blogger, a journalist or the manager of a website you'd like to submit to, hand them the sample and offer to follow up. These connections often happen at events, either randomly or through traditional stalking methods.

Be My Guest: Finding Great Guest Bloggers

When outside experts write for your blog, you add a new voice to your site, you add credibility, you leverage their social networks and *you get an article without spending the time and effort to write it yourself.* But you'll get few or none of these results unless you select your guest bloggers carefully.

The first two criteria should be obvious. You want great writers. They know their subject matter and they write posts with substance. They're skilled in crafting compelling content and they write posts with style. Read what they submit as if you were a visitor.

Ask yourself: Does the headline get your attention? Does the article hold it? Did you learn something from it? Would you be likely to comment or share it?

Social following, the third criteria for guest bloggers, is optional but highly desired: Do they have a large social following and are they willing to use it to drive some traffic your way? Look them up on Twitter, Facebook or LinkedIn. Some social media professionals use Klout, the somewhat controversial social media metric, to estimate online influence.

Ask yourself: Do they have an audience? Are they engaged within social channels? *(fig. 27)*

Two out of three may be ok.

Fig. 27

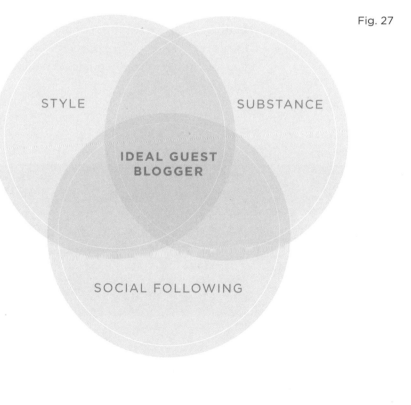

STYLE

SUBSTANCE

IDEAL GUEST BLOGGER

SOCIAL FOLLOWING

If they don't meet these criteria, you'll need to politely decline ("Sorry, but this post isn't right for our audience right now.") or give them an opportunity to improve it ("This is a little light / isn't quite strong enough. Would you like to add more specifics / edit it down / add more examples / submit something else?").

Guest Blogging Guidelines

If you are serious about guest blogger outreach, you'll save time setting expectations by providing guest blogger guidelines, either as a file you can share or a web page on your site. Guidelines are becoming common on popular blogs. In many cases these sites are adding contact forms on "Write for Us" pages so that visitors can convert into qualified potential guest bloggers.

The **outcomes of guest blogging** are virtually indistinguishable from the outcomes of PR.

The guidelines below are basically a shorter version of the Article Checklist in Chapter 4. Feel free to use this worksheet or your own guidelines based on your standards for content aspects and quality.

- **Types of Posts** - Ask for submissions that appeal to your audience and align with other content on your site. Posts should fit nicely within your blog categories.

- **Tone and Style** - Conversational, approachable, helpful, useful, interesting.

- **Length** - 500 words.

- **Formatting** - Encourage the use of headers, subheaders and bullet lists.

- **Images** - Suggest (or require) that they submit an image with copyrights and sized to the appropriate width for your site.

- **Search Friendliness** - Suggest that they optimize the article for a relevant keyphrase. Provide guidelines for writing search friendly content if available.

- **Author Box Info** - Ask for two to three sentences about the author along with links to websites and any relevant social media accounts (Twitter, Google+, LinkedIn).

- **How to Submit** - Require interested bloggers to provide their content to you in a format that makes it easy to review and post. This may be through a web form, in a Word doc, HTML, a shared Google Doc, etc.

- **Originality and Reuse** - Require that the content provided by guest bloggers is unique and has not and will not be used elsewhere. You want to have exclusive use of the article.

TIP! You should reserve the right to edit guest posts. If you do make changes, the guest blogger shouldn't mind. In my experience, it's very common for host blogs to make significant changes to my submissions, such as changing the headline. Do I mind? Not at all. Except when they add a lot of bad stock photos. :)

Your guidelines may also highlight the benefits of being a guest blogger on your site. Assure the possible writer of acknowledgement, a great link and new audience. Remember, these guidelines are intended to make communication more efficient and lay the groundwork for collaboration.

Guest Blogging = Modern Day PR

The outcomes of guest blogging are virtually indistinguishable from the outcomes of PR. Technically it is just one PR tactic, but as the news media revenue model continues to evolve, crowdsourcing of content becomes more prevalent, and publishing content becomes easier for blogs and brands, guest blogging will be ever more important for PR professionals.

Currently, guest blogging as a tactic falls into a gap between the skill sets of SEO and PR practitioners. Although SEO pros know the value of links, they don't have access to the powerful host blogs since search engine optimizers don't typically create content. PR pros can create compelling content, but they don't typically understand the tactics and benefits of link popularity. Social media pros may be the first to bridge this gap.

Try it. You'll find that the principles of guest blogging align closely with the philosophy of content marketing in general: create, connect, collaborate and help others. It's fun.

Inspiration: Content Genesis

Science is work, often requiring long hours of effort with uncertain outcomes. But it's also punctuated by eureka moments. As a content marketer, you'll have many of both.

Writing is a means of getting things done or promoting ideas. Actual scientists spend lots of time writing grants to get research funding. They're promoting their ideas through writing, just like any content marketer.

The inspiration for new content is part of the joy of content chemistry. Seeing a piece of content planned, created, promoted and measured is always satisfying, but for me nothing beats the big bang of a new idea.

Ideas for content can come from any direction. The more you write, the more open you'll become to new concepts. Also, the more you write, the more opportunities you'll have to repurpose content, as described in the Periodic Table of Content.

But if brilliance isn't forthcoming, there are many resources to trigger your imagination. In fact, there are so many "101 Ideas for Writing" articles, you could begin by writing a "Top 10 List of 101 Ideas for Writing" article.

Teach

If you haven't written the answers to these questions yet, write these first. These often become the "cornerstone content" that you refer to (and link to) from many other posts. The more likely you are to mention these topics in conversation, email and other posts, the more important it is to write this content soon.

These topics are often great for search engine optimization. People are always looking for practical information. And practical content is also some of the most shared.

1. What are the most important things that your audience should know before buying? Write a list post with a number in the headline. Use this as a subject line in an email newsletter. Also share it with prospects during the sales process.

2. What is your best advice? What is the right way to do the job? If there are several, make a list and use the number in the headline and subject line. Target keyphrases such as "[topic] best practices."

3. What question do people ask you most often? Write two versions, a short version for your FAQ page, and a longer one as a guest post. Link them to each other.

4. What question should people ask you, but don't? Make this post your best advice for your buyer with unexpected help during their decision-making process. Target keyphrases such as "How to find a [product/service]." This post can be shared with prospects in your pipeline.

5. Is it possible for your audience to solve their problems without your help? How? If there is a DIY approach for your audience, they'll find it. But if you don't publish it, they'll find it somewhere else. Write a practical guide in the same tone you would use if you were talking to a friend.

You'll gain more in followers, traffic and respect than you'll lose to DIY competition, especially if you target the right keyphrase. Try a phrase such as "how to [solve problem]."

6. What do people who are trying to enter your profession need to know? What's challenging about your job? What's rewarding? Although they may not be prospects, you may find an eager audience for your expertise in the next generation of professionals. These readers may remember you years later. Target keyphrases such as "tips for [industry] job seekers."

7. What is the last professional event you attended? What did you learn? List the things you learned at a recent event in a recap post. Mention the speakers or

> The inspiration for new content is part of the **joy of content chemistry**.

people with whom you talked. Share the post with these people once it's live. Share the post in Twitter, and mention people who actively used the hashtag during the event.

If the event will happen next year, schedule a Tweet to go out around the time that registration will open. If you use the hashtag, the organizers may see this and share the post with their network.

8. What are the tools you use everyday? What is the best way to use them? (Software? Services? Cement trucks?) Write a roundup of your top tools and techniques. Mention the brands that make your job easier. Use a number in the title and as the subject line in a newsletter. Mention the brands when you share it on social media. They may share it with their audience. Or if any of the brands have blogs and accept guest posts, submit it! Link back to a service page on your site in your author bio.

9. What is the one statistic that emphasizes the importance of your product/service best? Why is this stat important? Make a graphic of this statistic and use it as the featured image. The post should include some analysis about this number, why it matters and where it's going. Use the statistic in the headline and in your email newsletter subject line. Make sure the image appears when you share it in social networks.

Stories

List posts may get lots of clicks, but it's the stories that readers really connect with. Great marketers are great storytellers. These are questions you need to answer early and often. The personal tone gives them an advantage in social media. Some of these questions should be answered on key web pages, such as "About Us."

> List posts may get lots of clicks, but it's the stories that readers really connect with. **Great marketers are great storytellers.**

10. Why do you love what you do? This is your passion story. Link to this post from your bio on your website. Also, share this on social networks. Make sure to use an image that means something to you.

11. What is the unmet need of your audience? How do you meet this need differently than others? Give give an example. This relates directly to your brand's positioning. Link to this article in your email signature. Share it with prospects during the sales process.

12. What are the greatest successes with the best results that can be achieved by using your product or service? This story could be about any company who used the type of product or service, and not necessarily one of your customers. If the success is measurable, use a number showing the success in a how-to

headline, such as "How FruitCo. Sold 81% More Bananas with Guerilla Marketing." Use this as the subject line in an email newsletter.

If the story is about your service and your customer, make it a case study. Use specific details, quotes from the client and statistics. Make it a web page and also a PDF download.

13. Is there a risky (illegal or unethical) way to solve the problems that your company solves without the risk? What could go wrong? What's the worst that could happen? Use quotes and statistics to add emotion and credibility. Share it on social networks using dramatic excerpts from the article. Link back to your site so visitors can read the full story. These posts can also get traction in search engines. Target keyphrases such as "[topic] mistakes."

If you don't want to go negative on your own site, submit this one as a guest post to a popular industry blog.

14. How does one of your personal interests relate to your job? Find people in your industry who share this personal interest by searching Twitter profiles in FollowerWonk. Search bios using "[industry] [interest]," then mention these people in tweets to the post.

15. What relevant lessons could your audience learn from a famous person, movie, TV show, book or song? Write a post that makes the connection. The post will likely be both entertaining and insightful (example: "Web Design Techniques from Jean Claude Van Damme," written by our own Nick Haas). Find people in your industry who also enjoy that character, story or genre. Again, FollowerWonk will help (search Twitter bios for "martial arts" "web design").

16. When people use your product or service, what are some of the unexpected benefits or side effects? How are these things felt by the customer? Ask a thought leader in your industry for a quote or example. Add this to the post. Once the post is live, politely ask the thought leader to share it with their network.

17. Explain how you have changed your approach (or stopped doing something) since you started out in your industry. Create a chart showing changing industry trends. Make sure this image appears when you share the post in social networks. Or write a headline that uses the current year, such as "Underwater Archeology in 2013: What's Changed." Use this as an email subject line.

18. What industry blogs or magazines do you read? Which posts there get the most shares and comments? Can you add something to this topic? Submit your new article as a guest post to a similar blog that hasn't covered this topic. Link from the post to other pages on your site.

Interviews and Surveys

These are great formats for writers who are stuck, since it's as much curation as creation. The content produced has advantages when promoted in social media.

19. What are the blogs from which you've learned the most? What have they taught you? Contact the bloggers and ask if they would be open to a short email interview. Use the Q&A as the post and add some analysis, opinion and gratitude. Once posted, invite them to share it with their network.

20. What are the most fundamental questions in your industry? Create a short survey and send it to the largest group of relevant potential respondents. LinkedIn is a good place to find people. Partner with an industry association if possible. Package the results into a post and PDF with nice graphical charts. Make sure it's well designed. Share it with the respondents, leaders and industry publications.

Thought Leadership

Here's where you take a stand. To answer these questions, you'll need courage and strong opinions. Remove the softening words like "maybe," "probably" and "sometimes." Make bold statements. This voice carries on social media and helps online networking.

You may wake up the next day to long blog comments, new followers and a few detractors. Connect with the respectful, like-minded people on several social networks. They may become long-lasting contacts.

21. What question is no one in your industry willing to answer? If possible, submit this as a guest post to the most popular blog or news site in your industry. They might love the topic. If you post it on your site, check to see if the question is a popular search in Google. (Example: "why do banks charge fees" gets 590 searches/month.) If so, align it with this phrase. Long phrases, such as questions, are often less competitive and easier to rank for.

22. What does nearly everyone disagree with you about? Share the post with several social media influencers who don't share your view. Engage them in a conversation online, then share the post and politely ask for feedback. They may comment, share or refer to your view in a post of their own.

23. What do you believe will happen in the future that other people consider impossible or unlikely? Could it happen? You think so. But ask the question on Quora and in LinkedIn groups. Share the post on the other social networks. Politely email it directly to potential useful contacts. Within all of these conversations, build relationships with the people who respected your view. Keep in touch with them!

Idea Templates and Headline Hacks

There are a few simple arrangements of words that are so successful as headlines that they are virtual templates for ideas. Here they are:

[number] of [blank]
about [blank]

What [blank] can teach
you about [blank]

Source: Danny Iny (Copyblogger)

Just because these are formulas doesn't mean the content will be low quality. We've all read, enjoyed, learned from and maybe been convinced by articles in this format. They are extremely versatile and can produce targeted, easy-to-consume content.

Jon Morrow wrote a whitepaper called *52 Headline Hacks: A "Cheat Sheet" for Writing Blog Posts that Go Viral*. It's possibly the best collection of headline ideas available. It separates these template headlines into six categories:

- **Thread Headlines -** What Keeps Your Readers Up At Night
  Example: 27 Complaints about Web Design Companies

- **Zen Headlines -** Promising Your Readers a Simpler Life
  Example: Perfect Profile Pictures: 9 Tips

- **Piggyback Headlines -** Riding on the Back of a Famous Brand
  Example: What Lady Gaga Can Teach Marketers

- **Mistake Headlines -** Irresistible Teasers from the Masters
  Example: 15 Grammatical Errors that Make You Look Silly

- **How-to Headlines -** The Oldie but Goodie That Never Fails
  Example: How to Write When You Have No Ideas And No Time

- **List Headlines -** Bite Sized Content That Readers Adore
  Example: 52 Types of Blog Posts that Are Proven to Work

Here are some additional ideas for content that are specifically designed to take advantage of the chemistry between social media and search engine optimization.

Interviews

Interviews with experts add credibility to any website. Text-based interviews can be an efficient way to produce excellent articles. If you interview people who are influential, they may help promote your content through their social networks.

- Email an expert five questions.
- Email five experts one question.
- Invite fans and followers to ask questions on Facebook and Twitter. Have experts within your business write answers or answer questions on video.

TIP! Lee Odden recommends asking interview questions that include target keyphrases. If the reply includes the keyphrase, you may end up with compelling, natural-language content that is also search friendly.

TIP! Video interviews are more difficult to produce, but often very engaging. Just think of the size of the viewership for content producers like Conan O'Brien.

Follow the Leader

A little research can lead to a lot of ideas. It's useful to look carefully at what is already working, whether it's on your site or possible host sites when you're guest blogging. Once you've done the research, you can choose a topic and a format similar to the posts and articles that have already been successful.

- Look at your own Analytics to see the top posts and pages on your site. Which pages are most frequently visited? Where are visitors spending the most time?
- When guest blogging on other sites, look through the older posts on the blog. Which articles have the most comments, shares, likes and +1s?

Make a list of the most popular or successful posts, then start breaking them down. Do they have similar headlines? Topics? Tone? Now you can start to see what interests the site's readers.

Reverse engineer this high-performing content and you'll find patterns that new ideas can fit into. This will help you find that great idea by narrowing your options and considering the context. You'll also have a structure that makes writing much faster and easier.

Just pick a popular blog and find a post that has been successful based on the number of comments and shares. Break down the length of the post, the length of the paragraphs and the sentences. Listen to the tone of the writing. Look at the supporting elements: examples, statistics, images, quotes, links, mentions and calls to action. Deconstruct the formatting: headers, subheads, bullets and bolding. If you found the post by searching for a keyphrase, examine the keyword usage.

Now consider making your next article conform to these attributes. It's likely that in doing so, you'll be adapting your own piece, making it more concise, more conversational, more scannable, more shareable and more effective.

Attend Events

Every event that you attend is an opportunity to create content. Mentioning speakers or other attendees you meet will give you reasons to share the post with others. They'll be likely to share it with their networks. If event summaries aren't relevant to your audience, consider making this a guest post on another local blog or industry blog. If there's a website for the event, they may also be interested in posting it.

Look in Your Outbox

Here's a well known blogger trick for getting new ideas: reading old emails. Scan through the last few hundred emails you've sent. Are there any topics that come up consistently? These are good candidates for web content.

While you're digging through these emails, notice the tone of what you've written. It's probably informal and concise. This is likely the same tone that your website visitors would appreciate.

You may have great communication skills and email etiquette, so don't set that aside when you write an article. Keep using that simple language and a friendly voice. Don't suddenly start writing like a PhD candidate just because it's an article. Be yourself. Write like you're sending an email.

TIP! To keep the tone of your writing conversational, read your articles out loud to a friend when you're done. The jargon and formality might jump out at you right away. Or have an editor from outside your industry review the article. Another tip: Each time you sit down to write, put this at the top of the page: "Dear Mom…"

Email is also a constructive way to overcome your own objections to content marketing. If while reading this book, you've said to yourself, "I don't have time to write" or "I don't know how to write," just look at all those messages in your outbox. You're already a writer! You may already be producing 1,000 words every day on the same topics and in the same tone that you should use as a content marketer.

Write for Each Stage in the Conversion Funnel

Content works in many ways. Some writing pulls your audience toward you, building awareness. Other content builds trust, compelling your audience to take action. In other words, *content can be useful at strengthening different parts of the funnel.*

The "funnel" is just a metaphor for the path that visitors take on their way to becoming leads and customers, starting with awareness and ending with action.

Every buyer of every product and every service goes through a series of steps: *awareness, interest, consideration and then the action of actual transaction.* From the impulse purchase of a Tootsie Pop in the checkout aisle to the government purchase of radar installations, every purchase goes through this funnel.

For most buying decisions, the interests, questions and concerns of potential buyers are consistent, making it possible to define the funnel and then create content that aligns with prospects' interests and concerns.

Every great website first gives visitors the information they're looking for and then gently guides them toward the information it wants them to read. Ultimately, it leads visitors to the contact page and subsequent thank-you page. Content needs to support this process at every step. *(fig. 28)*

NOTE! If you have more than one target audience or type of conversion, you may need to create more than one funnel. Each type of visitor has a separate set of interests and concerns that should be addressed with separate content. For example, one funnel may be for lead generation while a second funnel may be for newsletter subscribers.

Fig. 28

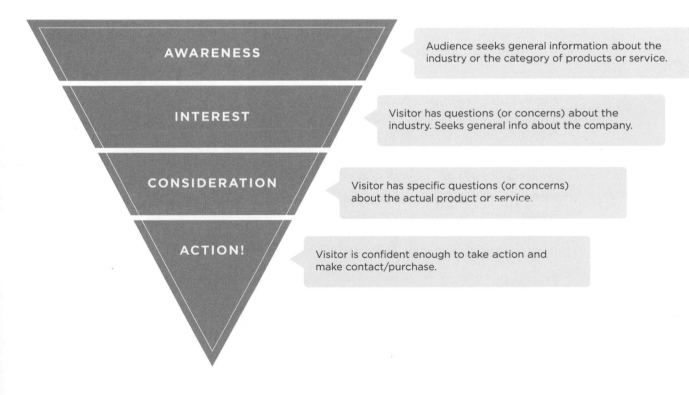

AWARENESS — Audience seeks general information about the industry or the category of products or service.

INTEREST — Visitor has questions (or concerns) about the industry. Seeks general info about the company.

CONSIDERATION — Visitor has specific questions (or concerns) about the actual product or service.

ACTION! — Visitor is confident enough to take action and make contact/purchase.

Top of the Funnel: Awareness

Goal: Get attention, establish relevance to the topic, branding.

If your conversion rate from visitors into leads is good (above 2%), but traffic is low, the top of the funnel is weak. Here are some tactics and topics that will help...

Search-friendly blog content

Traffic from search engines is an excellent way to fill the funnel at the top. Research keywords before writing your next post. Aligning posts with keyphrases is the fastest way to fill the funnel.

Guest blogging

Guest blogging offers three benefits to the top of the funnel. It grows your social following. It improves your link popularity, making your site more likely to rank. Finally, it strengthens your network of allies.

Shareable, cross-platform content

Of course, you should be sharing everything across all of your networks. Better yet, adapt your content to perform well in other places. Fill your social streams with visual content that pulls visitors toward your site. Make that post a video and post it on YouTube. Turn it into a presentation and put it on Slideshare.

List posts

Some posts get more clicks than others. Numbered lists tend to get more clicks because they set an expectation with potential visitors: they're organized, scannable and there are multiple items that may be useful or interesting.

Middle of the Funnel: Consideration

Goal: Educate, engage, get visitors to go deeper and to subscribe and follow.

Your site has few shares and no comments. Traffic from campaigns is low and the email list isn't growing. Very few visitors return to the site and the average visitor sees less than two pages. *These are signs of weakness in the middle of the funnel. Try these tactics and topics...*

Write detailed, authoritative posts and pages

Visitors love "how-to" posts that are truly useful. They demonstrate expertise and position your brand as helpful. These are the posts that compel visitors to subscribe and follow, and those actions lead to repeat visitors.

Link together related topics with relevant content

If your website has detailed pages about topics A and C, but not B, then visitors may leave to find that information elsewhere. Ask yourself, have you missed something? Write those pages and link them to the related pages.

Collaborate with relevant influencers

Build credibility by partnering with people whom your audience trusts. Contribute to relevant blogs and invite relevant bloggers to contribute to your site. This collaboration is a form of endorsement that strengthens the perception of your brand.

Use a personal tone, be approachable

Building a community means being a person. Visitors should be able to hear the voice of the brand in the writing. They should see faces in the team section. They should see interaction in the comments. Faceless companies just aren't as memorable.

Bottom of the Funnel: Action

Goal: Turn "suspects" into prospects, build trust, inspire visitors, start a conversation.

If the conversion rate of your website is below 1%, you've got a problem at the bottom. If it's not a complicated lead-generation process or confusing ecommerce checkout, the problem is probably the content. These tactics and topics support the bottom of the funnel...

Stories that show your values

If lists are for the top, stories are for the bottom. Take your time and tell the complete story of why you do what you do. The story should show that you care and that the work you do makes a difference, whatever it is!

Show evidence of the value of your services

Use data to prove your results. Numbers can be powerful motivators. Also put the voice of your customers throughout your site as testimonials. Anything you write is marketing. But when someone else says it, it's social proof.

Content that answers the most common sales questions

For every prospect that contacts you and asks a question, there may be 100 others who didn't even bother to reach out and ask. Listen for those common questions and publish the answers on your site.

Guide visitors from the blog into the marketing pages

A great marketing blog gently steers visitors toward the marketing pages. The posts should be relevant to your products or services and link to them within the text. These links guide visitors deeper into the funnel toward conversion.

Calls to action relevant to the posts

Are you suggesting that people connect with you? Is there a call to action at the bottom of pages and posts? Or is each page a mini dead-end? Nudge visitors toward your contact page with quick calls to action throughout the site.

Articles for specific prospects

You have a few potential clients that just aren't ready to sign that proposal. Do they have specific concerns? Are several of them worried about the same thing? Quickly write a post, case study or white paper that addresses that concern. Even if it doesn't close the deal, publishing this may warm up the next lead.

TIP! For larger organizations, *the marketing team and the sales team can collaborate.* Once the marketing team finds out what questions are being asked during the process and what concerns prospects have, new content can then be created to fill gaps in the funnel.

Online Networking Guide: 35 Ways to Connect with Anyone Through Social Media

They're big names. They're influential. They have an audience. You know who they are. And it would be great if you could connect with them.

But how can you network with these influencers?

Here is our guide to online networking. It's a step-by-step approach to using social networks to build the relationships that will power your marketing. It's the relationships with influencers that lead to press mentions, shares, links, rankings and traffic.

> **PRO TIP!** If you're looking to use social media to drive search engine rankings, read: *How does social media affect SEO?* http://www.orbitmedia.com/blog/how-does-social-media-affect-seo/

Back in the day, there were three ways to connect: in-person (knock, knock), the phone (ring!) and US mail. Today, thanks to social media, there are a lot more. And each little action is visible and can bring you closer together.

Here are all the little actions you can take to become visible to – and eventually become friends with – any influencer.

First, Let's Find Some Influencers

If it's obvious who you're trying to connect with just skip down to the next section.

Generally the influencers who can benefit us the most are those who create content. These are the people who can mention us publically. So we're looking for:

- Bloggers and blog editors
- Journalists and authors
- Podcasters and radio hosts
- Event producers

We're going to find them online, which is easy since social media is the world's greatest phone book. We'll start with Twitter since it's filled with influencers.

1. Search for influencers (and content creators) on social media
The Twitter Advanced search tool isn't great, so I often use FollowerWonk. The key is to search for keywords that include your topic or industry, plus the word "blogger," "writer," or "journalist." *(fig. 29a)*

The search results should include all kinds of influential people in your industry, sorted by the size of their Twitter followings. It also shows their "social authority." Although this isn't a very reliable metric, if an account has a social authority of one, it's probably a robot or fake account.

2. Build a List
You should have 20 or more potential networking targets. You will be more likely to succeed if you don't focus on just one or two accounts. Every good content strategist maintains several lists: topics, keywords,

guest blogging/PR opportunities and influencers!

Now let's get on with the process of ~~schmoozing~~ slowly making friends.

Start Listening: Get Their Content

If you're not paying attention to someone, why should they pay attention to you? So the first step is to put the influencer fully on your radar.

3. Subscribe to their newsletter

Simply sign up for their newsletter or add the feed for their blog to Feedly. Feedly is better because you can put all the influencers in a category and watch them separately. This also keeps the noise down in your inbox.

I have them in a category called "Watch List." Now I can see them all in one place and I'm more likely to engage with their content. *(fig. 29b)*

4. Comment on posts on their blog

Now you can start interacting with their content through comments. Every writer reads their comments, so it's an easy way to make them aware of you.

5. Like their comments

If their blog uses LiveFyre or Disqus for comments, you may have the opportunity to like their comments and responses to other comments.

Next we'll move on to the social networks. Here's where you're going to start interacting in small ways, building up to a full-on friendship.

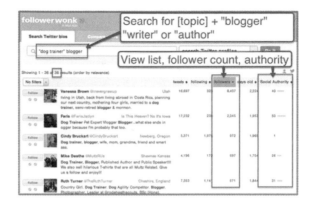

Fig. 29a

Fig. 29b

6. Put their name into Talkwalker and Newsle

These tools will email you when your influencers get mentioned in news sources. These might be press mentions or guest blog posts that you'd miss if you only subscribed to their newsletter.

Twitter

This social network is the bread and butter for building relationships. Here are the steps involved.

7. Follow them on Twitter

8. Add them to a "Radar" Twitter list If you're following more than a few hundred people on Twitter, then it's likely that your home stream is very noisy. So you're unlikely

to see the tweets of the influencers you just followed. This is where lists come in.

Create a list called "Radar" (or name it something flattering, such as "People who write great stuff") and add the influencers there. Make it a public list so they can see that you've added them. Next add that list as a stream in HootSuite or any other social media management tool.

Now the tweets of these influencers will be more visible to you and you'll be more likely to read, retweet, favorite and mention them. *(fig. 29c)*

TIP! Use "Link Listening" to find any Tweets containing a link from a specific site. It's a simple and highly effective strategy for any business using content marketing for lead generation. You can read the full article on "Link Listening" by Robert Moore on Spin Sucks. http://spinsucks.com/social-media/business-social-listening/

Fig. 29c

These next steps should be done many times over several months.

9. Retweet their content

10. Favorite a tweet

11. Mention them in your tweets

Google+

It's an underrated and active network, not to be ignored. Even if it seems quiet to you, there are still hundreds of millions of people to connect with, including influencers in your niche.

12. Add them to a Google+ circle

This is similar to adding them to a Twitter list. Put all of your influencers into a circle so you can watch them all at once. This makes it easier to watch them specifically and take actions that make you visible to them.

13. +1 their posts

14. Comment on their posts

15. Mention them in your posts

Next we're ready to move on to the higher levels of online networking.

LinkedIn

Everyone in this social network is there for the networking. But it's never the place to start. When you invite someone to connect, they have to accept your invite. Cold connection requests sent to influencers are often ignored.

Don't add the person until you've already built up some awareness with them.

16. Connect on LinkedIn

17. Endorse on LinkedIn

18. Mention them in an update

19. Write a recommendation

A LinkedIn recommendation is actually very valuable, so it's a very nice thing to do for someone. The person you recommend is unlikely to forget the favor. And as long as it's genuine, there's nothing wrong with recommending someone, even if it's just for their writing.

Facebook

Like LinkedIn, Facebook friendship requires confirmation. But since it's personal as well as professional, this is one of the last social networks to use. Don't click the "Add Friend" button unless you have built up awareness to the point that confirming you as a friend is an obvious decision.

20. Send a friend request on Facebook

21. Like their Facebook posts

22. Mention them in an update or comment

If you're not making friends, you're doing it wrong.

Even though you're on Facebook, don't get too personal. Remember, you're networking. So keep it professional and non-creepy. Nobody likes a stalker.

Other Networks

There are actually hundreds of social networks and places to connect. The influencers you're networking with may be on many of them.

23. Follow on Quora, Instagram, Yelp, MeetUp, Listly or anywhere else!

24. Follow on apps

Beyond websites, apps are often places where people connect. Are they a runner? Maybe they're on RunKeeper. Are they a music lover? Maybe they're on Spotify. Once you're truly connected, it's not strange to connect in many places.

Here's a technique that makes it easy to build many connections to the same person…

Cross the Streams

Connecting on one social network just isn't enough. An easy way to become more visible to someone is to jump across social networks during a single interaction. We call this "crossing the streams." Here's how it works.

Step 1: Influencer mentions or shares your content within social network A.

Step 2: You share the content again in social network B.

Step 3: In the share, mention the influencer, thanking them for sharing it earlier.

When you mention the influencer on social network B, you'll become visible to them there. If they share it once, this may trigger a second share from them on this second network. More importantly, you are now more likely to connect with them in another network, strengthening the connection.

The more connections to the influencer the better. So that's the next step in using social media networks for relationship building…

25. Thank the influencer in one network for an action in another network

Example: How to Cross the Streams

a. Make blog post live, share and promote it aggressively

b. After several days, check Topsy to see who shared it on Twitter. (more tips on how to use Topsy http://www.orbitmedia.com/blog/how-to-use-topsy/) *(fig. 29d)*

Fig. 29d

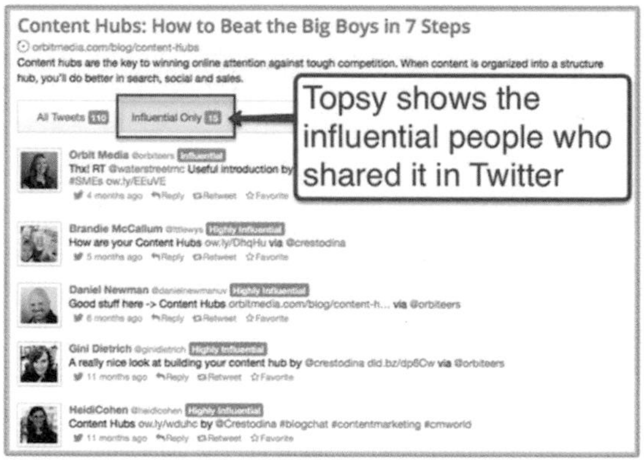

Fig. 29e

c. Share the post on another social network, such as Google+ and mention the influencers, thanking them for their shares and comments on the post. *(fig. 29e)*

Your Blog

Remember, if you've got a blog, you're a publisher, which gives you a chance to give ink to others. A blog is a networking tool.

26. Mention them in your content

Find a quote from your target influencer and add it to your content. Go beyond a simple quote by adding a few things to it.

• Add a thoughtful note

• Link back to their content

• Add their picture

Once it's live, mention them when you share it and thank them for inspiring you. You might make their day!

You get what you give.

If you ever want to be mentioned in someone's content, mention them in your content first!

Offline Networking (this is how the pros do it)

Social media experts don't keep it online. They move the conversation offline whenever possible. In fact, your best social media tool is your phone.

27. Phone call, Skype or Google+ Hangout

It's real-time and it's powerful. Can you really say that you're friends with someone if you've never had an actual conversation with them? End that long string of emails, pick up the phone and dial.

I do Hangouts with bloggers from around the world on a regular basis. The request sounds like this:

"Your stuff is great and I'd love to learn more from you. And there may be a few tricks I've learned that I could show you. Do you have time to jump on a quick G+ Hangout next week?"

If you've built up the relationship properly, the answer will likely be yes.

28. Meet in person!
This is why coffee was invented. An in-person, face-to-face meeting is the highest value interaction possible.

I value in-person meetings so much that I actually have office hours every Wednesday, Thursday and Friday at 8am. I meet with anyone and talk to them about any topic. I've met hundreds of people this way. The networking benefits have been huge.

Industry Events

This is my secret weapon for networking. Events are a great place to learn, but they're also a fantastic place to network. I can't list all of the bloggers, editors and influencers I've met at events. This is not an exaggeration: most of the opportunities I've had in marketing came from connections I made at events. Events have been huge for me.

29. Go to industry events where your favorite influencers are speaking

30. Take a picture with them, share it on social media and tag them

Events are also a good place to meet event directors who book speakers for subsequent events. If you'd like to speak at an event, it's a good idea to go once as an attendee and meet the organizers while you're there.

Write Reviews

Authors and podcasters all prize one thing above all others: reviews. They are hard to win and worth a lot. This is why virtually every podcast ends with a friendly call to "head over to iTunes and leave us a review."

If you're networking with an author or podcast, score huge points with these two actions.

31. Amazon Review

32. iTunes Podcast Review

Collaborate on Content: Email interviews

This goes beyond just quoting them in your blog posts. In fact, working on a piece of content together may have been the goal of your entire outreach effort. Collaboration may be a final step in the networking process before you ask for something big.

Regardless, once you've work on something together, you'll be better connected forever after. Here are the three main ways to collaborate on content using email interviews.

33. Invite them to contribute quotes
Get a special contributor quote from them and include it in an article.

34. The Expert Round Up
Roundups are a ubiquitous format for content for a good reason: they're interesting and they get shared a lot. Readers love them and they're great networking.

35. Deep Dive Interview

Go deep into a topic by sending them a list of questions. Or send one question at a time and make the post more conversational.

These types of collaboration aren't just good networking, they're a type of ego bait that may lead to them sharing the post with their social followings. That can give you a little traffic boost.

Fig. 29f
Source: Groove

Anatomy of A Relationship-Building Email

This has resulted in an 83% positive response rate and infinite invaluable feedback.

Fig. 29g

The "Ask" with an easy tweet link

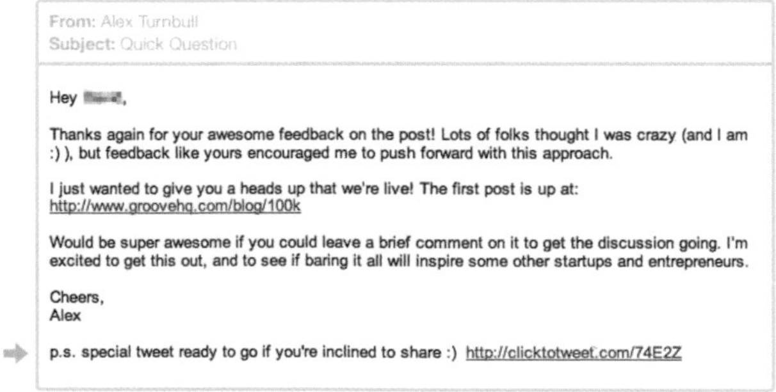

Finally, The Big Ask

If the goal of your networking was to eventually ask the influencer for a favor, such as write about us in your newspaper or please share this article with your audience, then here are a few tips on how to structure the email.

This is a two-step process outlined by Groove on how to send a relationship building email and the following up with "the ask." *(fig. 29f)*

After they respond, the second email includes the request, which in this case was to comment and share. *(fig. 29g)*

You can see the approach: friendly, concise and easy.

Why it Works: The Reciprocity Bias

At the heart of this strategy is a predisposition built into all of our brains: reciprocity. If someone does something for you, you are automatically predisposed toward doing something for them. It's called the reciprocity bias.

We naturally feel a sense of obligation after we receive something. It's a cultural imperative in every society.

So all the little actions we take in social media are ways to genuinely connect. To meet and connect with people that you have a real affinity with. But all of those nice things you do will gradually increase the likelihood that the person will do something nice for you.

The Fame-to-Speed Ratio

The more famous the influencer, the more patience you'll need. If they have a following much larger than yours, go slow. The more similar you are in levels of authority, the faster you can go through this process. *(fig. 29h)*

Here's an example of some power networking from the 1960's with master promoter Jerry Weintraub.

"When I was in my twenties – I wasn't successful at that time – I had a dream one night and I saw a billboard saying "Jerry Weintraub presents Elvis Presley at Madison Square Garden." The next morning I called his manager, Colonel Tom Parker, and said I wanted to take Elvis on a tour. He said no. I called him every day for an entire year and we had the same conversation every morning. Finally, I got a phone call from him and he asked me whether I still wanted to take Elvis on a tour. I said yes, very much so."

Since Elvis was one of the most famous people of his generation, a daily phone call for a year was necessary. But it worked. That's persistence!

Fig. 29h

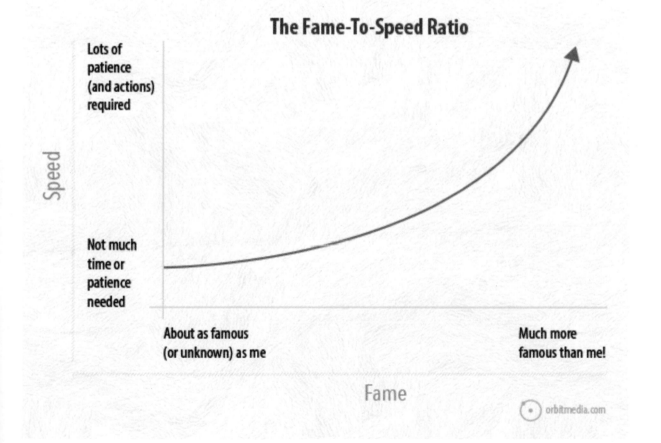

The Fame-To-Speed Ratio

Speed

Lots of patience (and actions) required

Not much time or patience needed

About as famous (or unknown) as me

Much more famous than me!

Fame

orbitmedia.com

Conclusion

So there you have it. You should now have a good understanding of how websites succeed through traffic and conversions. You should also know how content helps achieve these goals.

Ideally, at this point, you're excited to start mixing things up in the lab. You're ready to experiment with keyphrases, discover new connections and concoct a big batch of relevant articles.

Persist

Yes, it's going to be work. There is no secret formula. Content marketing isn't about just one thing. It's about 100 little things. And it's about doing these things well and doing them consistently. It may take time to find the style that works for you and gets a reaction from your audience. You'll need to keep at it if you're expecting big results. Persistence is the biggest factor in success, not just in web marketing but in every field.

"Marketing is a habit, not an event."
John Jantsch, Duct Tape Marketing

You'll see small results right away - a few shares, more clicks, some new people accepting your invitation to be added to your list - but it will take time before you become an expert.

Some of the greatest content chemists of our time put in tremendous effort to get where they are. It took Chris Brogan 8 years to get his first 100 subscribers. Today he has hundreds of thousands of readers each month. Lee Odden of TopRank Online Marketing has written more than a million words during his career. Today he's one of the most sought after web strategists in the country.

You don't need to work for 8 years to get 100 subscribers or write a million words to get results. Thankfully, there are plenty of small incremental results to measure along the way. But it will take patience and effort. Keep going; you'll get there.

Fear Not

Almost nothing is as high-stakes as it seems. Yes, there are examples of spectacular failures in social media. There are nightmare stories of collapsing search engine rankings. But these stories are rare relative to the millions of businesses doing content marketing.

> "Fortes fortuna adiuvat."
> Fortune favors the bold.

Don't be afraid to try something new. Don't be afraid to write something provocative. If an article rubs a few people the wrong way, there are probably hundreds of other people who appreciate the candor. If you feel strongly about something, let it show through your words.

Have fun!

To me, web marketing is a game. I play it like a sport and Analytics is my scoreboard. I've chosen certain metrics that I like best and I try to make them move. It's actually easy to gamify your marketing because there are so many beautiful charts to look at! Thinking of it as a game, and making those charts and numbers move helps keep me motivated.

Everything you're about to do is measurable, and the results of your efforts make lovely charts. So pick out a few statistics and watch a few of the charts. Choose the ones that have an impact on your goals and start obsessing over them a little bit. Call it a "key performance indicator" if you want. Personally, aside from leads, some of my favorite stats are: newsletter subscribers, newsletter click-to-open rates, Google +1s

> "**Marketing is a habit**, not an event."
> JOHN JANTSCH, DUCT TAPE MARKETING

and total visitors. If these numbers are growing, results will come. I'm always trying to break my high score.

So I watch the charts. I measure. I wonder. I tweak. I try something new and I measure again. And somewhere along the way, I forget that I'm working. I'm having fun.

If you're not having fun, you're doing it wrong.

Resources

A lot of things in this book are likely to change over the next few years. There are new social media tools, new ranking factors in search engine algorithms and new trends in what visitors expect from websites. Keep learning.

MORE ADVICE! The Orbit blog has posts on many topics that weren't covered here. We invite you to drop by to read our latest content marketing advice. You can also stay connected through our newsletter and social media:

www.orbitmedia.com/blog/

twitter.com/orbiteers

plus.google.com/+Orbitmedia

www.facebook.com/orbitmediastudios

Here is a list of some of the resources that I've used over the years to learn many of the things in this book. Many of these I still use every day. One of the wonderful things about content marketing is that the experts are all happy to teach what they know. They do it every day on their websites, in their videos, in their newsletters and at conferences.

I'd like to both thank and recommend the following websites and thought leaders. Believe it or not, I've never met any of them. But they've each had a profound effect on me. I'm grateful and, by way of thanks, I encourage everyone to read, watch, follow and subscribe to these wonderful resources, as I have.

- Moz/Inbound.org and Rand Fishkin
- Copyblogger and Brian Clark
- HubSpot and Dan Zarella
- TopRank and Lee Odden, author of "Optimize" (highly recommended)
- Marketing Profs and Ann Handley, co-author of "Content Rules" (another book I am constantly recommending)

Here are some other superstar websites and experts I recommend taking a close look at, in no particular order:

Liz Strauss, Joe Peluzzi, Nick Kellet, John Morrow, Danny Iny, John Jantsch, Ross Hudgens, Ian Lurie, Danny Sullivan, A.J. Kohn, Jay Baer, David Meerman Scott, Chad Pollitt, and John Carlton.

Also a huge thanks to my partners and fellow content marketers here in Chicago, from whom I've learned so much, including Mana Ionescu of Lightspan Digital, George Zlatin and Taylor Cimala of Digital Third Coast, Brad Farris of EnMast, Gini Dietrich of Spin Sucks, and to Tim Frick and Jill Pollack, my partners in ContentJam, our content marketing event. This includes Tim Frick of Mightybytes and Jill Pollack of Story Studio. Thanks to my designer, Bridget Gannon, who made this book look beautiful. And to my editors, Amanda Gant and Kim Bookless, who showed such persistence and clarity, making this book so much better and keeping me on track.

Lastly, thanks to my business partner Barrett Lombardo as well as Todd Gettelfinger and the rest of the Orbiteers. The work you do every day for our beloved clients is an inspiration to me.

Notes

Notes

Notes

Notes

ANDY CRESTODINA is a co-founder and the Strategic Director of Orbit Media Studios, an award-winning 40-person web design company in Chicago. Since 2001, Orbit has completed more than 1,000 successful website projects. The Orbiteers combine talent and experience in developing beautiful, effective sites for businesses in every industry.

As a top-rated speaker at national conferences and as a writer for many of the biggest blogs, Andy has dedicated himself to the teaching of marketing. Over the past 15 years, Andy has provided web strategy and advice to more than a thousand businesses. His favorite topics include content strategy, email marketing, search engine optimization, social media and Analytics

Andy graduated from the University of Iowa with a degree in Asian Language and Literature, and a certificate to teach Chinese. Today, he lives and works in the tree-filled neighborhood of Ravenswood with one cat and his lovely wife, Crystal.